The Sweet Spot

The Sweet Spot

The Moments That Can Transform an Ordinary Life ...
into an Extraordinary Experience

BO PICKLESIMER

Published by Best Seller Publishing®, St. Augustine, FL
Best Seller Publishing® is a registered trademark.
Printed in the United States of America.
ISBN: 978-1-959840-29-9

For more information, please write:
Best Seller Publishing®
53 Marine Street
St. Augustine, FL 32084
or call 1 (626) 765-9750
Visit us online at: www.BestSellerPublishing.org

For now we see through a glass,
darkly; but then face to face:
now I know in part; but then
shall I know even as also I am known.

1 Corinthians 13:12

Contents

Part Two

Part Three

Preface

WHEN I WAS A very young boy, not much past my fifth birthday, I discovered one of my mother's most treasured possessions. As I recall, in appearance it seemed to be just a plain wooden binder held together by three leather strips. Imprinted upon the outside front cover were some decorative markings that left one with a subtle impression of simplistic beauty.

The specific details of those markings have long been erased from my mind. For it was not the cover design that was to leave the lasting impression; it was the treasure found within. A source for memories never to be lost.

Contained inside the wooden covers of that binder were a number of pages. There must have been twenty or more of those heavy card-stock sheets found within that family photo album.

On each side of each sheet were displayed six or more black-and-white photographs. Each of the photos was held in place by four glued-on corner holders. I don't recall a particular sequence relative to time or another clear theme as to how those photos had been arranged on those pages. I was too young to think about that at the time. I simply enjoyed immersing myself in revisiting the images each time I picked up that binder. As I would turn the pages, it was as if I were reliving moments in time, in a life that I had never lived. It never failed to bring on a strange sensation.

The first time I heard the song "In Color" by country singer Jamey Johnson, the memories of the hours spent turning the pages of that small wooden binder came flooding back. The lyrics tell a story about revisiting moments of the past. In the song, though the living of those moments had been in color, the visual evidence had been captured only in the dull black-and-white images of a time long ago. I could relate to the lyrics because I had discovered a fabric of my parents' lives in the same way.

On rainy days, the hot days of summer, or on the very coldest days of winter when the freezing temperatures kept me inside, I would occasionally find myself sitting on the stuffed couch in the front room of our house, just poring over those photos. They were photographs of family members and friends, in a variety of settings and poses. Most reflected the earlier lives of people I knew. Some of the older photographs were of people I had never met—and would never know in this life. All of them were snapshots in time, the forever capturing of a moment, never to be seen or lived again. I felt a certain sadness that accompanied my viewing of those photos. It was a feeling of loss, of having missed something that could never be retrieved.

We often think and measure time by the hours, days, months and years, but life is really about the moments. When we reflect and search our memories, we may be taken to a particular period of time in our lives, but our thoughts of the telling of the story always instantly move to the moments. Just as it appeared on the pages within that small wood-covered picture album, the moments of our lives are just like images captured by a camera. If it's true that a picture tells a thousand words, the snapshot of our moments has the same power. It's in those moments where we find the stories that can help bring a fuller appreciation of, and meaning to, our lives.

Life cannot be condensed into a photo album. But somehow the photos found on those pages, within the covers of that plain wooden binder, impressed upon me at an early age that life is fragile and not to be taken for granted. Once a moment passes, it is gone forever, living on only as a memory.

This is a book about stories … the moments. It's a book about the potential for change that can come as we experience those moments and take the time to search out their meaning for us.

One of life's challenges is to not let the moments slip by unnoticed. If we are paying attention, the opportunities come each and every day for us to experience a very special place … that place, a moment I like to think of as the "sweet spot."

Introduction

I RECALL HAVING A conversation with my mother in her later years. I had called her up just to check in. Well, that's not exactly true. It was the time in our lives when I knew that she wasn't going to be around forever, and my call that day was one of a number of calls that were made with a purpose. I was trying to make sure that any unanswered questions were answered before it was too late … before the day came that she would no longer be there to pick up the phone.

The call with my mother on that particular day became another reminder of the need for having the conversations … and the taking of some time to do the remembering.

Our lives unfold with nearly all those moments eventually lost to us and others. How many untold stories exist that should have been preserved but which silently slipped unnoticed through the cracks of time and into eternity? I have lived long enough to see it happen to too many people, too many times.

On those calls with Mom, we would do a little reminiscing, have a few laughs and occasionally shed a tear or two. Actually, it was usually me doing the shedding of tears. That is what conversations with your mother will sometimes bring. There was some recounting of stories that involved family, friends and acquaintances. Some of the best moments were when we were revisiting an experience that she and I had shared ... just the two of us. It was all good.

In one of those conversations, I asked her about a particular experience from when I was very young. It was one I remembered well, and I looked forward to just one more revisiting of that piece of our mother and son journey. It came as a shock to me that she had no memory of it and could not recall anything relating to a moment in my life that had made such a significant impression on me. How could that be?

One thing I have come to understand is that some of the moments that may have been so significant for each of us may have been less significant for, or gone completely unnoticed by, others. I once came upon an old high school classmate whom I had not seen since our school days. Strangely enough, though I recognized and remembered him, he seemed to have no memory of me.

It is true that time can play tricks with our memory. It had been more than twenty-five years since I had last seen my classmate. I later learned that he had suffered a stroke, which may have affected his ability to recall past events. However, perhaps it was simply a case where our interactions were just more significant to me than they were to him.

No matter the particular circumstances that challenge our recollection of memories, the years have a way of robbing us of many of the moments we would choose to remember. This was my takeaway of that one conversation with my mother. I had lived long enough to know that she was not the only one who was challenged with recalling events. I took note.

Actually, I literally took note. I began to work at documenting significant moments in my life. It began with my jotting down words or short phrases; anything that could help bring past experiences to mind. Eventually, it evolved into more detailed notes, with a number of those remembrances becoming short stories … pages out of the book of my life. Along the way, I discovered that there were three Rs that I was using to help me fully appreciate the experience of the moment: Reflection, Recognition and Reconciliation. Each of them play a part in turning every moment of one's life into something more than it might have been.

So, this is a book of stories, not fabricated or written for inclusion in a novel … just the stuff of life. An interesting side note is that, as I have on occasion shared some of these stories with family and friends, their recall has varied regarding the recollection of some of the details. Any experienced trial lawyer can relate to this, as it is fairly common for multiple witnesses under oath to offer varying and conflicting testimony in the recounting of a singular event. I have come to appreciate that the lessons to be learned from the moment are more important than the total recall of the details. Maybe that is one of the lessons of life, in and of itself.

I read somewhere that more than a million books are published every year. Does the world really need another one? I guess I will let you be the judge of that. I only know that after that conversation with my mom, there had to be at least one more.

More than a few years have now passed … time stops for no one. It's been a while since there has been anyone to answer Mom's phone when I call. She's no longer with us. I miss those conversations and reminiscing with her … the shared reliving of the moments.

I like to think she would enjoy the retelling of these stories just one more time. My hope is that you might, in some way, find them as meaningful for you as they were to us. I know Mom would like that.

Part One
Reflection

THERE ARE A NUMBER of lessons I learned from my dad in my youth. One of the most significant of those was my observing his habit of pondering—the giving of thoughtful consideration to a particular subject or topic of interest.

I recall on occasion that he would share the discovery of some bit of knowledge that he had attained. It was interesting to me how he seemed to take pleasure in the process of coming to understand and share something that was previously either unknown or less understood. In retrospect, it seems to me that for him, these revelations always came after some period of reflection.

An example of that would be a thought he shared with me in the latter part of his life. He had come to understand that every decision he had made that involved a move to relocate our family had changed every day thereafter. Each family member's life was forever different than it would have been. Like the stone thrown into a body of water, where the initial impact generates wave after wave of changing of the surface, so are the choices of our lives. One decision forever impacts everything that follows. Everything.

I am sure that Dad's periodic observations sometimes came in the form of epiphanies. However, in retrospect, more often it was his habit of pondering and taking time for further reflection that brought about a fuller understanding and appreciation of life's learning moments.

In my youth, I learned to love the game of baseball. I particularly loved standing in the batter's box and having my turn at facing the opposing pitcher. Perhaps the best part of the game was the pitcher's throwing of his best pitch and the accompanying taking of my best swing. With my bat meeting the ball in just the right way, I would feel the "perfection of the connection" moment. The result was a feeling that everything was happening in that moment exactly as it was meant to be. Sweet.

Just as there is a "sweet spot" in the game of baseball, there is that same kind of thing in life. It is there when we feel the moment of connection … the feeling that something has come together in a way that touches us, has the power to change us and help us better understand this thing we call life.

Whether the connection with the "sweet spot" on a baseball or one of life's special moments of learning, it is all the same. For me, experiencing those moments began in the earliest days of my childhood. An understanding and appreciation of the value of the reflection process would be learned along the way as I came to better understand that "pondering thing" Dad had taught me by example.

Stones thrown into the water … one day at a time.

Appalachian Education

I WAS BORN IN Eastern Kentucky. Most people wouldn't recognize the small town where my life began. I just tell folks I spent some of those early years of my life living partway between Mud Lick and Flat Gap.

If you are not from that part of the country, you probably wouldn't know there are two Kentuckys. The central and western parts of the state are known for a number of things ... the region's bluegrass, horse racing and the Kentucky Derby, and the winning tradition of University of Kentucky basketball. Eastern Kentucky is in a part of the United States known as Appalachia ... beautiful mountains, some of the best coal in the world, and poverty.

For many folks in that region, life can be hard … real hard.

Most of the memories of those first years of my life spent in Appalachia are good. When you are a child, life can be simple and uncomplicated. A child shouldn't have to worry about having a roof over their head or food on the table. I later came to understand that this is not true for everyone. Fortunately for me, the days of my early childhood were mostly full of just looking for ways to entertain myself, with much time spent roaming the hills and exploring the hollers.

Family was the common denominator in many of those early childhood memories, with my grandparents and many of my aunts, uncles and cousins living in close proximity. I had many "happy days," long before actor and producer Ron Howard came along in the '70s and made those words a household term with a popular television sitcom about the '50s.

The one notable exception to all the good memories was my first introduction to that thing we call death. Though many others would follow, those first experiences left lasting impressions. Often the education in your life begins well before your first day of school.

It was in my fifth summer that my dad brought home a beagle pup. Every boy and girl should have that experience: the joy that comes from the playful interaction and the relationship that develops between a child and their companion pet. There is a reason dogs are known as man's best friend. If shown attention and love, a faithful dog responds in kind multiple times over, and a lasting bond develops. I have experienced and observed it many times.

As it always happens, the warm and playful months of summer gave way to the changing of leaves on the trees as the fall season came along. Being a young boy, I barely noticed the gradual shortening of the daylight hours, along with the arrival of the cooler changes in temperature. Having little experience with the cycle of change that comes with the seasons, winter arrived almost without notice. It was to be a memorable one.

There was little insulation in our house, and the coal stove in the front room was our primary source for heat. On the coldest days, hours were spent with a blanket and staying warm by finding a spot as close to that heat stove as possible. When you are young, all your experiences can be first-time lessons, and the coldness of that winter became one of those.

After one particularly cold night, Dad came back into the house the following morning to tell us that my "little pup" had not survived the night; with the extreme cold, he had frozen to death. He had been bedded down with a blanket and box-covering in our outdoor shed, but the cold had just been too much for him.

I don't recall any outpouring of emotion over the event. I was old enough to understand what had taken place. Death is always final. I was too young for thoughts of second-guess recriminations, and I somehow knew that questions of judgment could bring about no change. As a child, you come to understand that things happen, but in those moments, there is no answer to the questions of why. The fact is, there is just no way to alter the outcome once the verdict is delivered. What I had no way of knowing, at that moment, was that I was soon to experience more loss.

At that time, our next-door neighbors were also our landlords. Junior and Dorothy were a couple, probably in their late fifties, but they seemed much older to a boy as young as me. Their home was more nicely furnished than the one we rented from them. One of the obvious defining comparative features was the outdoor privy. Theirs was a comfortable structure, with the interior finished something more like the inside of a home. Ours was constructed of rough-hewn timber, inside and out. We did, however, have one benefit that was unavailable to them. Growing near our back door was a small peach tree. The peaches produced by that tree were some of the most delicious I have ever tasted!

I really don't recall any interaction I would have had with our neighbors prior to the event that was about to take place. In somewhat the same way as the loss of my pup had been announced, I learned one morning that Junior had taken his own life. Unknown to most who knew him, he had fought an ongoing battle with alcoholism and depression. The day came when he could no longer go on, and he put a gun to his head.

Shortly after, there appeared a grave on the hillside above us that was a constant reminder of that loss. In the coming days, my mom spent many hours comforting Dorothy, our neighbor. I would occasionally accompany her on those visits. On more than one occasion the grieving wife remarked that she just hoped that she would be able to see her husband again.

My mother had not been raised in a way where she had developed an understanding, or faith, in the afterlife. So she was unable to provide any comfort regarding the widow's plea. However, her sister had found a faith that taught the principle that families could be together forever. In prior conversations, my mom had shown no interest in learning more about her sister's newfound faith. Now, in the hope of being able to help a grieving neighbor, she reached out to her sister for answers of comfort.

That inquiry, and subsequent conversations, became not only a source of comfort for a grieving neighbor but also led my mother to a path of conversion that changed her life and the lives of many others. The change of faith for my mother was most providential, as it would not be long before she would be confronted with a most unwelcome challenge and share a similar need as that of her widowed neighbor.

At that point in time, our family consisted of my parents, myself and one younger sister. But Mom was expecting an addition to our young family, and we were all eagerly awaiting the arrival of that little one. There was no reason to think that the birth of this child would be any different than my parents' experiences with my sister and me. But that was not to be the case.

Complications arose in the delivery process. Healthcare facilities were not what they would later become, especially in Appalachia. Our newborn sibling lived less than a day. A picture of my sister and me standing graveside with my little brother's casket is the lasting memory I have of that sad experience. My parents were heartbroken.

It was many years later that my mother shared with one of my sisters that, on that first night after she came home from the hospital, she waited for my father to fall asleep before allowing her tears to flow. That was so much like my mother—to carry as much of the burden as possible, to help lessen the pain of others.

Likewise, in the moments following Dad having told his mother and father of the loss, my grandfather found my father at the dining room table, sobbing, head in hands. The only comfort Papaw could offer was the thought that there must have been a purpose in not having my brother survive the birthing experience.

I don't think there was anything that had prepared my parents for the experience. No modern-day parent expects to bury one of their children. For me, I had lost a brother. Perhaps the loss of a neighbor and my little pup were experiences given to help me prepare for the loss of a sibling. Sometimes we think, or may say, that we know what another person is going through. But we really have little idea about that unless we have walked that mile in their shoes. We can acknowledge it, but it is impossible to feel it in the same way that they are.

I was eventually to have another sister and three more brothers, but this little brother would be the one I would not get to know in this life. He wouldn't share some of the joy of the experience with us, but he was also spared any of the hurt and pain. He is the one who just wasn't able to stay as long as the rest of us. Only God knows why.

So, the introduction to death was a part of my early education. But there was a much more significant lesson I took from those earliest years. Like much of the learning that comes with this life, the full appreciation would not come until years later, after many experiences and much reflection.

In those early years, our family had little in the way of material things. Our small, four-room home had no indoor plumbing. The tin roof over our heads provided cover from rainstorms but, with little insulation, could not keep us comfortably warm when the winter snows came. Heat was provided by that coal-burning stove in the front room and a small potbelly stove in the kitchen.

We drew our water from a well, both for drinking and bathing. After heating the water on the stovetop, we took our baths in a three-foot-wide stainless steel tub. For obvious reasons, it was always preferable to be the first one to bathe. Trips to the outdoor privy were of little inconvenience most months of the year but could be unforgettable experiences in the dead of winter.

We ate mostly out of our garden in the summer months, with soup beans and cornbread a staple during the remainder of the year. The variety in our diet was fairly limited, so any deviation tended to be somewhat memorable. A nickel candy bar or a small bag of M&M's had the potential to become an unforgettable moment of pleasure.

I will never forget the taste of the first cheeseburger I experienced. I was probably four years old. I had ridden the bus to town with Granny, my dad's mother, and we had lunch at the G.C. Murphy five and dime store grill. I remember the circular stool Granny sat me on and, after all these years, I can still recall the sensation of the taste of an ice-cold Coca-Cola and that cheeseburger. I have never had a more enjoyable meal than the one I shared with my grandmother that day.

Years later, Mom recalled that after the rent and utilities were taken care of, we basically lived on ten dollars a week. Despite the losses experienced and having little in the way of the things money could buy, those early years were some of the happiest of my life. Down the road, other losses, disappointments and challenges were ahead. For me, the foundation had been laid in understanding that, no matter what, it was up to me to make my life what I could make of it. I could choose to be happy or choose to be sad … and having "things" had little to do with the feeling that would accompany my choice.

Too often we waste our time and energy in search of that next thing that we think will make us happy ... the new job or promotion, the new house, the car, the boat, the next trip or vacation or the next relationship. How is it that so often, when we experience that next thing, we find ourselves empty and unfulfilled, still searching for something more?

That's something I always try to remember when I find myself looking forward to, or wanting, that next "thing," the one thing that I think is going to make me happy ... but never does.

Fire in the Hole

THE MINING OF COAL was one of the chief occupations in those mountains of Eastern Kentucky.

The hillsides of my grandparents' homestead were mined for years. I have often marveled at how my uncles were resourceful enough to make a living bringing that coal out of the ground. Working beneath the surface with little more than a four-foot-high ceiling, they would work their way deeper and deeper through a hillside seam of coal.

Shooting the coal was hard and dangerous work. As young boys, my cousins and I were repeatedly warned regarding the dangers when we found ourselves around one of the mining sites. I remember well the specific warning about the blasting caps that would ignite the charges of dynamite and loosen the mother lode of coal.

But there were other dangers in those hills to be concerned with, and I was to become intimately acquainted with some of them early in my childhood.

My parents seemed to have been blessed with a healthy baby boy as their firstborn child. Nine pounds-plus at birth and active, I was abandoning crawling and learning to walk in my ninth month. But it wasn't long after taking those first steps that something happened … something changed. My mom noticed I had begun walking less and crawling more as I moved about. Soon thereafter, I stopped walking all together. Something was terribly wrong.

Upon examination and testing, it was determined that I had contracted spinal tuberculosis. The more common form of TB affected the lungs and was a killer as it attacked one's respiratory system. The form of the disease I had was attacking my spine and making it impossible for me to stand and walk. My parents were told there was little hope for treatments or cure. For most, only the therapy of rest was practiced, with the hope for eventual recovery.

Dad was serving in the Air Force at the time, so I was fortunate to have the care of military physicians. With access to only the local health services, the attention I would have received would have been limited. Under those circumstances, I would most likely have been left with a different outcome than the one I was to ultimately experience.

To secure the rest therapy for one so young, my spine was immobilized by placing my body in a plaster cast. From just below my shoulders to just above my knee, I lived day-to-day in that cast for nine months. There were consultations at that time of possible surgery to fuse my spine, but my parents were hesitant to take such a drastic step, as that would have had a debilitating effect on me for life.

Fortunately for me, an experimental drug had been approved and was being administered to patients like myself. The "medicine" came in the form of a sweet syrup, with the instructions that I should take a prescribed dose of one tablespoon a day. As I found the taste much to my liking, I would often sneak a second dose.

I am not sure whether it was those extra unprescribed doses, or just the much-needed immobilization and rest for my back that provided the cure. Whatever the reason, following nine months of being in that body cast, and with the aid of a back brace, I was once again able to walk. I continued to take doses of that syrupy mixture as my recovery to better health continued. After several years of annual follow-up visits to the specialists, I was cleared of any physical concerns.

Though I will always test positive for tuberculosis, I have been able to live a completely normal, healthy life ... the only possible effect being that I am an inch, or more, shorter than my brothers. However, that might have something more to do with genetics, as my mom and her father were both short in stature. In retrospect I consider that whole experience as the first miracle I was blessed to experience in my life. But there have been others, and the next one came just a couple of years later.

The dangers to health posed by the use of tobacco were less known in the 1950s. The habit was not only socially acceptable but was also promoted in all forms of the advertising media of the day. Smoking was a fashionable trend prominently on display in both television programming and on the silver screen.

Closer to home, it was also something that I experienced in my family interactions on a regular basis, and I found it more than slightly distasteful. So much so that I recall as a small boy dreading the day that I would become a grown-up and have to learn how to "enjoy" smoking a cigarette.

I really couldn't understand what made the habit so appealing for my parents, aunts and uncles. However, there was one redeeming aspect of the experience that never failed to catch my attention. It was the use of that shiny chrome object that adults would hold in their hand, an almost magical tool which had the power to create … fire.

The thrill of it all probably goes back to the days of cavemen. There is something about fire that is fascinating … especially to young boys. I have had a couple of stints as a scoutmaster with the Boy Scouts, and the common predominant interest of boys on campouts is the campfire. I once returned with the troop from a weekend camp, and at our Sunday morning service, our bishop asked if one of the boys would like to give a report to the congregation. I gave the assignment to John, one of our troop's patrol leaders.

At the appointed time, John was called forward. His report was brief and to the point. He shared that the weather had been good and the troop had had a great time. "We built a big campfire and burned up everything we could get our hands on." I always felt that the boys thought I was a good scoutmaster, but the parents might not have been of the same opinion, especially following reports like John's.

I guess, in retrospect, I was a little ahead of my time relative to those kinds of experiences with fire. One day, using as much discretion as a four-year-old could muster, I stole away to what I thought would be a good hiding place where I could experiment with that shiny chrome cigarette lighter. I secreted myself behind an end table by the sofa in the front room of our house, excited and in full anticipation of discovering for myself the mystery of "making" fire. Having observed it happening on a number of occasions, I quickly found out for myself how surprisingly easy it was for me to repeatedly have that lighter ignite and bring a flame to life. But then, what to do, now that the art of creating that flame was accomplished?

As I sat in my secret hiding place, looking around, I noticed that right behind me were the curtains that covered the large window in our front room. It took no more than a moment to have an interesting thought come to me. What would happen if I were to place the flame near those curtains?

What in the world makes a four-year-old have a thought like that? That may be another one of those mysteries of life that cannot be explained. Before I took the time to give any thought to the possible consequences, I found myself once more igniting the flame and holding it next to the nearest curtain panel.

As the flame touched those linen curtains, to my shock and horror, it rapidly began to spread upward. Almost without any hesitation, I folded the curtain over itself and extinguished the flame. The momentary relief I felt was quickly replaced by another kind of terror, as I realized that my brief experiment with fire had left a four-inch hole in the curtain, accompanied by an ugly extended scorch pattern. The damage done left me with an immediate realization that this could not go unnoticed by my parents. My fate was sealed.

Even for one so young as myself, I knew there was absolutely nothing that I could do to escape eventual detection and some form of punishment. A "switching" with a freshly cut willow branch was the usual punishment, but I thought for something as serious as this I might draw a heretofore unknown form of discipline. At that moment, I shuddered to consider what might be more painful than several willow branch switch strokes across my bare leg.

As I looked back on this event years later, the conclusion that a miracle had occurred on that day is inescapable. As a four-year-old, I had no knowledge relative to the properties of fire. In my previous experiences, I had seen fire created, but I had no understanding of how to extinguish it. My reaction at that time had been instantaneous, and the only course that could have prevented a disastrous outcome. Another miracle followed later that day when the damage was discovered by my parents and I escaped any severe punishment. I guess my folks were just thankful I hadn't burned the house down to the ground.

Some of my early childhood experiences helped prepare me to believe that there was more to life than mere happenstance. Along the way I have come to believe that miracles, great and small, happen for a reason and they happen every day ... if we expect them and are paying attention.

Maybe whether we notice miracles and see them for what they are is dependent upon whether we come to see God's glass of life for us in this existence as being half-full … or half-empty.

That journey to seeing the "half-full glass" always begins with the "blasting cap" of faith … along with a humble recognition, and acceptance, of God's hand in our lives.

Zoo Animals, Chewing Gum and Jesus

PLAYING WITH FIRE WAS not my only childhood misstep. A life of crime could have begun for me at an early age. That is how it usually happens. A person makes a choice that starts them down the wrong path. Sometimes that first wrong choice is like a domino chain, with one bad choice leading to another. At a very young age, I had an experience that could have put me on that sort of path.

It was sometime after my third birthday when I had my first brush with the law. I hadn't been exposed to a gang. I didn't even have any idea what a criminal was. Nevertheless, when I committed my heinous act, I knew it was wrong. How my mother handled the situation at that moment was to leave a lasting impression. It would be my first lesson in being accountable and taking responsibility for my actions.

Mom instilled in me a love of reading at an early age. On our weekly visits to town to buy groceries, I was often allowed to pick out a small children's book to bring home. The evidence of that regular occurrence was reflected in a stack of books that accumulated in the corner of a small playroom in our home. That stack must have included fifty, or more, "Golden Book" volumes that my mom read to me over and over again. Those books included an assortment of traditional fairy tales and stories, along with the retelling of many of the popular television programs and Walt Disney movies of the day. When properly organized and stacked, my storybook collection stood at least a head or two taller than me. The weekly visits to town were a continual source for the building of my childhood library.

However, one day, on one of those weekly visits to town, something other than a book caught my eye. It was a plastic bag of colorful play figures—zoo animals: lions, tigers, monkeys and so on. I knew the moment I saw that little bag of animals that I had to have them. But my hope of taking them home with me that day was dashed when my mother refused to place them in her shopping cart. In retrospect, it didn't have anything to do with her not wanting to make that day the happiest day of my young life. She probably just wanted me to have another book added to my playroom library, not some bag of toy figures.

As my mom went about her shopping that day, I quietly slipped away and made my way back to the aisle where that beautiful bag of colorful zoo animals was displayed. I don't recall taking any length of time debating my next course of action. The die was cast the moment I left my mom's side.

No amount of questioning the right or wrong of what I was about to do was able to stop me from removing my heart's "desire of the moment" from the toy display rack. With my treasure in hand, I made a quick exit from the store and found my way to the back seat of our parked car. The thrill of opening the bag and holding those zoo animals in my little hands came with feelings of guilt. I knew I had done something wrong. However, at that early time in my life, I was not capable of making the connection between choice … and consequence.

Little did I know that my first introduction to that inevitable law was just around the corner.

I hadn't been playing with those little plastic animal figures very long when Mom found me and immediately went about teaching her son one of the earliest lessons of his life. I was marched back into the store and introduced to the store manager. What had taken place was explained, with the attending appropriate apology offered on my behalf. As my mom paid for that bag of zoo animals, I thought that what I wanted more than anything else was now mine. I was also in possession of my mom's first moment of disappointment in a son that no amount of money in my little piggy bank could have covered.

There was now something that made those small, colorful figures a whole lot less desirable. The thing that I had wanted so badly never became a favorite toy that I could really enjoy. How often we find the shiny object that attracts our attention isn't quite the same thing once we have it in our possession.

Strangely enough, my son was about the same age when he had a similar experience. His desired treasure was a package of chewing gum that screamed "Take me!" as we stood in the checkout lane at our local grocery store. Somehow his mom and I missed seeing the little guy pick up that pack of gum and stuff it into his pocket.

To his horror, the very next day as he returned home from his half-day of kindergarten, he discovered that the "crime" had been uncovered by his younger sisters. Scattered all across his bedroom were a variety of colorful gum wrappers. His treasure of chewing gum had not only mysteriously disappeared and was nowhere to be found, but the bigger concern for him was that his criminal indiscretion could no longer go unnoticed by his mother. The first lesson in honesty and accountability came early for my son, just as it had for me. More opportunities for learning were to follow.

It was a few years later, as our family was seated at the dinner table one evening, when we became aware that our son was struggling with a bit of a moral dilemma. However, the real problem was that he wasn't struggling with it at all.

The issue had once again been brought to our attention by a sibling. This time it was one of his older sisters who disclosed the crime in progress. Our son, now eleven, had been doing some business on the internet. He had a "product" that he was marketing online and a customer who was dissatisfied with his purchase. The customer was a young boy. His name was Jesus.

As we became aware of the circumstances, the situation was one where our son had assembled an informational listing that he was marketing. The buyer had misunderstood the exact nature of the offer. Jesus was requesting a refund.

There was not a significant cost incurred in creating the purchased item in question—just some time in developing the "product" and listing it for sale. The problem was that our son didn't seem to be inclined to refund the young boy his money.

At that moment, no amount of reasoning on our part could sway our son's position on the matter. He felt justified in the position he was taking. I told him he wasn't being fair in addressing his customer's concerns, and in a moment of frustration I said, "Son, you can't cheat Jesus." Well, it wasn't really cheating, but I thought the statement played well in the argument. In the end, my son felt he was being fair, and Jesus didn't get a refund.

Many years have now passed since that family conversation at the dinner table. My son continues to enjoy being in business for himself. A significant piece of his company business involves T-shirt sales online. I called him one day, and during our conversation he updated me on how his business was doing.

With what seemed to be some amount of pride, he shared that he had a large box of T-shirts in the corner of his production room. He noted that this was the box where he tossed his rejects—printed shirts that had some flaw that he felt made them unsellable. He also indicated that in that box were the occasional product returns, when, for one reason or another, the buyer wasn't satisfied.

I inquired with some concern as to what cost this box of rejects might represent, and what percentage of his business sales ended up being flawed production pieces or customer returns. He responded, again with a note of some pride in his voice, that the percentage was relatively low, but there was a consistent cost of doing business relating to production problems and customer satisfaction.

I was left with the impression that my son felt, in the big picture, the cost was small when compared to the importance of satisfying the customer. He related that he had become very particular about the quality of production and admitted that there were times when some shirts ended up in the reject box although the customer probably would not have had any concerns.

Appreciation of the lessons of life can come with time and moments of reflection. It's interesting to me how similar experiences have come to both my son and me, ones that have provided opportunities to better shape our understanding of the importance of both honesty and accountability in our business dealings with others.

The intervention of caring parents often saves their children from all sorts of problems. Sometimes, the guidance, timely counsel and appropriate disciplinary actions are necessary to ward off choices that can have the obvious, more immediate disastrous consequences. Other times, it's just the stuff of zoo animals and chewing gum.

I think my son would agree that both he and I are still works in progress … and I would like to think that somewhere out there is another Jesus, who hasn't given up on either of us … along with everyone else in this world of ours.

Dad, That Little Round Ball and Me

I WAS THE OLDEST boy cousin on my dad's side of the family, and so I had my moments in the sun. I enjoyed being the "chosen" one for as long as it lasted and am not the least bit ashamed that I took full advantage whenever I could.

I had only one cousin who was older than me. Cheryl was her given name, but like so often happens when we are young, she ended up with a variation of the pronunciation. The "back in the hills" version came out something like "Shurry." She was a petite thing, a bit frail due to some dietary allergies, but full of energy and confidence. We were best buddies. I may have thought of myself as the king. But Shurry was the queen, and you know how often it is that a woman sharing the throne ends up being the ruler. Shurry loved to take charge, and often did. I didn't mind. She was the big sister I never had.

Our house was on a small but steep hill, with Shurry's house located across the road at the bottom of the hill. We would talk back and forth to each other nearly every day and would play together as often as our moms would allow.

One late summer afternoon, my cousin excitedly announced that she would soon be starting school. I was still a year away from being old enough to join her, but I didn't like the idea of not being able to share in this new adventure. As kids so often do, Shurry suggested that I should just ask my mom if I could begin my schooling a year early so we would be in the same grade … and so I did. Mom thought that would be just fine; after all, my dad's three oldest brothers had all started school the same year. So, come September, I found myself riding on the big yellow school bus with my best buddy as we started the first grade at Flat Gap School.

I don't remember at the time having any understanding that just a few years earlier my dad had graduated from the very same school. Grades 1 through 12 shared the same campus in those days. So, I was unknowingly wandering some of the same halls and grounds that my father had, not much more than ten years earlier. My first-grade classroom was located in a newer addition that had been built adjacent to, and at the back of, what was the main building. But the old cafeteria and many of the outbuildings that served as classrooms were still in use at that time.

A large playground and field were located behind the school. There was the large swing set that could be found on every school playground and a flat area where two old basketball goals had been planted in the ground many years before. But most of my fun memories I can recall from that time and place are of my classmates playing Red Rover. I loved that game.

Our teacher would divide the class into two groups. Two lines would be formed about twenty yards apart. The lines faced each other, with everyone in each group holding hands. There would be just enough space between the two lines for a first grader to be able to get up a full head of steam running. We would then take turns calling out to the other group, inviting one of their members to run and try to break the chain. The invitation would be a chant that went something like "Red Rover, Red Rover, send Shurry right over." If the runner was able to break the chain, they would take one of the other group's members where the break occurred, and have them join their own group. In the event that the runner failed in their attempt, they became a member of that group. The objective was to end up with more members in your group at the end of play. I don't recall anyone ever getting hurt playing Red Rover, no small miracle, but there was the occasional sore wrist.

Though the iron basketball hoops on the playground did not make much of an impression on me at the time, something else about that school did. Occasionally, in winter and on rainy days, our teacher would take us to the gym for an indoor activity. Walking onto that beautiful wood floor was like entering another world. It seemed immense, and there was a sense that it was a very special place. Looking back now, there was a feeling that it was almost something like hallowed ground. Though I didn't really understand all that happened in that space, I was as much in awe as any little five-year-old boy could be.

In retrospect, that gymnasium was much like a scene out of the movie *Hoosiers.* A regulation roundball floor with little space between the concrete walls and the out-of-bounds perimeter lines, wooden stands on one side of the floor for spectators, and a well-appointed curtained stage that served as a platform for special occasions made up the primary elements of the space. The two glass backboard goals at each end of the playing floor stood in stark contrast to the rusty metal backboard goals found on the outside playground court. At the time I had no idea that in this same space, just a few years earlier, my dad had experienced some of the best moments of his life playing a game that he came to love.

I grew up knowing very little about my dad's "playing" days. I was aware from photographs that he had been on the high school basketball team and later played on teams when he was serving in the military. For a time, as I approached my teen years, I was also aware that he played in a league with the guys at work. Sometimes my best friend and I would ride into town with Dad, hoping for a chance to play if one of the teams needed an extra player. I do not recall that ever happening. So, my friend Greg and I would always end up shooting hoops outside on the school grounds until dark, and then slip into the nearby L&K diner and enjoy a milkshake.

Years later, Dad helped coach me and some of my friends in our church basketball league. He would give us instruction on how to play the two-one-two zone defense, watch for fast-break opportunities, move without the ball and make a "no-look" pass. These were all fundamental elements of the game he had learned as a young player. I could sense that it was frustrating to him that we boys, along with many players of the day, did not appreciate the value of some of what his coach had taught him in the formative years of his playing days. I must admit that I did not fully appreciate all that he was trying to share with us at the time. Years later, I came to better appreciate all of it as I continued to enjoy playing and occasionally do some coaching.

For many young players, a coach can leave lasting impressions. Dad was the beneficiary of that kind of experience. He first began to develop some interest in the game of basketball playing with his younger brother, John. They would use an improvised ball and hoop out in the yard at their home. It was probably not there that Dad attained dribbling skills, as they would use make-shift objects for balls and the playing surface of the yard was uneven. But I can imagine that it may have been there where he first developed some skill at maneuvering, working his way to the hoop and experiencing the thrill of watching the ball drop through a little round hole.

By the time Dad was approaching his high school years, he had the benefit of some physical attributes that would enhance his playing skills. He was growing toward his eventual height of something approaching six foot two, which was tall for that time, and he had a lean, long build, well suited for the game. His senior year team photograph reflects a young man who has what I came to know as the serious "game face" look.

Dad had the good fortune of being coached by a man who was ahead of his time, relative to the game of basketball. Sid Meade had been exposed to something more than the usual high school game of the day, having been around some college coaches whose tactics were advanced for that time. Fundamental to the game that he preached was conditioning that allowed constant movement without the ball, passing, and the art of the fast-break. There may have been nothing that Coach Meade loved more than a great no-look pass, along with the good head-fake move, with the play ending in a close lay-in bucket.

One thing I observed about my dad is that he always enjoyed learning how to do things. Coach Meade was one of the early mentors in his life where learning occurred with significant results. As Dad moved through his high school years, his playing skills and love of the game evolved, and Flat Gap High School became a team to be taken seriously.

Good coaches like good players, and it seems that Coach Meade developed a special liking for my dad. He referred to him as "Big Pickle." Mondays, after weekend games, would always be a time in his history class for a recounting of the most recent game. At that time in his life, Dad may have been more dedicated to the game of basketball than he was his school studies. His coach had probably been cut from the same cloth.

But basketball wasn't Dad's sole, or most important interest, as was illustrated in one of those classroom recountings of the previous week's games by Coach Meade. It seems that as the team was about to go through the usual pregame warmups, Dad had the misimpression that the visitors had brought their reserve team along. Thinking he had some free time before the varsity game, Dad was making the best use of that time by giving an attractive girl, who would later become my mother, his undivided attention.

Unbeknownst to him, the bouncing balls he could hear in the gymnasium were not the reserves warming up but his varsity teammates. With the game about ready to begin, a team member was sent to find Dad. In the coach's retelling of the moment, as the game was about to start, Big Pickle was outside the gym and had a game of his own going on.

When I was growing up, Dad never shared many stories from his high school years, so I wasn't aware of the reasons he perhaps wasn't inclined to press me harder about my lack of good study habits and the need to excel in attaining better grades. Another story, told to me many years later, sheds some light on that subject.

It seems that Coach Meade had given the class the assignment to research a historic figure of their choice and be prepared to give an oral report. It was understood that the longer the report, the better the grade. As is often the case, some of the girls in the class were the more dedicated students and, as one might expect, they worked diligently to fulfill the assignment. One by one, day after day, class members stood and shared their reports. Coach Meade, in the role of teacher, would sit at his desk and, following each report, pick up his red marking pencil, pause to consider the grade to be assigned for the student, and mark it down in his class grade ledger.

Several of the girls in the class presented well-prepared, lengthy reports on their chosen historic figure. Following each of their reports, they all received an "A" grade for their effort. Dad's report was the last one to be presented. As Coach Meade announced that Big Pickle would be presenting his report the following day in class, he did so with a little chuckle. He knew his player well and was probably aware that Dad, no doubt, put more time into his playing than he did his studying. Expectations probably were not high for what would be shared in the upcoming presentation. Dad would not disappoint.

In his recounting of the incident, Dad remembers little about that report, only to say that it lasted only a few minutes. Following the presentation, as he took his seat, Coach Meade went through his usual routine of pausing to ponder and consider what the appropriate grade to be given might be. After what seemed an interminable interlude, he smiled and noted that he thought Dad's report deserved an "A" grade.

Now, perhaps the coach's giving of that grade was, in part, some kind of reward for what Dad was achieving on the basketball court or some consideration that he had to substitute a lot of his study time for basketball practice. It may also have been, in the awarding of that grade, that Coach Meade had in mind a memory of when he was in the classroom as a student, where he also may have been giving attention to some things other than his studies. Then again, maybe he was just having some fun aggravating those girls.

It was said by some that Dad was the best player to ever play basketball at Flat Gap High School. Some of his exploits are documented. He was recorded as having played in the county all-star game, having his scoring and play contribute to the team's win. There was a memorable game where Dad scored more points than the opposing team's point total. The Greyhounds didn't win every contest, but they came out on top most of the time. They beat Paintsville, the larger city team in the area, and made it to the state regionals that same year, losing to a good Pikeville High School team.

A humorous story is told of Coach Meade taking the team over to Grayson to play a larger county school. Prichard High School had both a basketball team and a football team, which was unusual in those days. They had scheduled their first game with Flat Gap with the thought that they could have a good start to their season by crushing a small-school opponent.

The game score went back and forth, with the contest in doubt to the very end. There were numerous questionable calls, with Coach Meade doing some ranting on the sidelines as he worked the officials. He played it a little close, nearly being ejected on a couple of occasions. The temper of the partisan crowd was evident as they witnessed a win slipping away in the final moments of the game. With just a few seconds left on the clock and Flat Gap looking to come out on top, the coach called a timeout. He said, "Boys, we may win this one, but we better get out of here quick when it's over." As the game clock expired, the coach had another win, and the team made a quick exit.

Years later, Coach Meade developed a colorful reputation as a high school referee. Like many men, as he aged, he had developed a considerable midriff paunch. His antics as he called games became legendary in the region. When play infractions occurred, he would blow his whistle and make various dramatic moves and gestures to accentuate the call. Some folks found as much entertainment in his refereeing as in the games themselves.

One of the stories told about him involved a game he was refereeing in a small mountain community. By halftime, the underdog visiting team had built a sizable lead over the hometown team. It was later said to have happened that Coach Meade was approached by a couple of locals at the halftime break. One of the men intimated that their team wasn't used to losing games on their home court. As the man made that comment, he made a motion that left the impression that he had a handgun in one of his bib overall pockets. It wasn't surprising how the home team was able to have a great second-half comeback and end up winning the game.

After I finished up high school, Dad and I were playing together on a city league team, when one of those memorable kinds of situations developed. We were playing a team of "tough boys," and there was little hope of coming away with a win. They had run us off the court in an earlier game in the season, beating us handily. Everyone was expecting a repeat performance.

In the first half of the second meeting, we were playing well, as we were doing some of the things that Coach Meade had taught Dad's high school team to do so many years before. We found ourselves in the locker room at halftime with a two-point lead and had the feeling that the boys in the other locker room couldn't be too happy about how the game was going.

We weren't so sure that winning that game might not come with some cost, as we came to the conclusion that we might possibly win the game but lose the fight afterward. In the second half, despite some concerns about any possible post-game activity, we gave it our best shot but ended up on the losing end by two points. We should have lost that game by twenty points, so I always considered that a "win" for us, especially since we were able to walk away without experiencing any physical harm.

In my youth, I came to love the game of basketball. I learned some of the game from playing with my friends and school teammates. I watched and tried to mimic some of the best college and professional players of the day. LSU's "Pistol Pete" Maravich and Earl "the Pearl" Monroe, one of the best guards to ever play in the NBA, were two of my favorites. I loved watching the Pistol make the "behind the back" pass look easy, and the "fall-away" shot ending one of the Pearl's penetrating drives to the basket was simply a thing of beauty.

But the tempered passion that my dad would have on display, as he would try to have me understand some of the finer points of the game, left the most lasting impression on me. In later years, I wondered how he had become such a good player. He had the benefit of a good coach, but in his high school playing days, he never had the opportunity to watch a college or professional game. Having reflected on that, one day when I had the opportunity, I asked him how he had been able to learn to play the game so well. He simply replied, "I always just did the best I could."

The game of basketball can present many lessons for life, and Dad had discovered one of the best ones as he was learning to play the game. And so, it was from my dad and the game with that little round ball that I learned one of the important lessons of life: you can't always be on the team that ends up with the winning score, but you have always "won" if you have just done the best that you possibly can.

It's a lesson that I always try to remember every time I walk out onto the "floor" to play my next game.

Brought-Ons

GET USED TO DIFFERENT.

As we walk along the path of life, we all come to understand that we are not exactly like everyone else. One of the most amazing things about this world is that, out of the billions of people populating this earth, there is no one exactly like you. What an incredible gift—that we are all unique creations.

However, instead of embracing and celebrating the ways in which we are all unique, we tend to be less accepting of those who are not like us. Reconciliation of "different" requires effort on our part. The truth is, most of us generally like our interactions and relationships to be easy, smooth and trouble-free. It seems to be our nature to gravitate to those who we are more like and separate ourselves from those with whom we have less in common.

My first introduction to "different" came to me as a small boy. Mom had taken me into town for an afternoon of playing at the city park. While working hard at enjoying the large sandbox in the middle of the playground, I noticed that one of my playmates had hair unlike anything I had ever seen before ... braided locks with all kinds of colorful ribbons. I asked my mom why my little friend's hair was so different, and she simply explained that her family were "Turkeynobbers."

A knob is Appalachian slang for a rounded hill, or mountain. The one family of color in our community lived on Turkey Knob. In absence of anything other than casual interaction, that was the way that family was given identity by some members of our community. In my innocence, from that encounter and for the first few years of my life, I was left with the impression that all people of color were "Turkeynobbers."

It was just a few years later that I experienced my own version of being recognized as "different." Dad had finished his associate tech degree schooling, and we had moved from Eastern Kentucky to Dayton, Ohio. My world changed overnight, and some of the change was very hard. On more than one occasion, I cried myself to sleep, as I was missing family and all the familiar surroundings of the only world I had previously known.

My folks rented the furnished second floor of a farmhouse from an older couple, Mr. and Mrs. Brosey. Their children had grown and moved out on their own, so we used most of the upstairs as our apartment. The furniture could be described as spartan, the bare necessities. One of the rooms was a converted kitchen with an antique oven and refrigerator. There was a living room and one bedroom. In retrospect, it was a very humble abode, but it was an upgrade from our Kentucky home, as we now had indoor plumbing.

Our entrance would be a walk through our landlords' kitchen to the steep interior stairway that led to our residence. We didn't have a telephone and would occasionally ask to use the Broseys' phone when that need presented itself. In some ways, we were almost an extension of their family. They were a kindly couple of typical midwestern stock. Their family farm was located just outside the edge of town and had all the things that a small boy could enjoy exploring. I could be found doing just that, hours on end.

It was many years into my adult life before I came to understand that, for the better part of our time there, Dad did not have a regular job. His recent schooling had trained him in the field of electronics, and upon arriving in Dayton, he had visited a local television repair shop for possible employment.

The owner sent Dad out on a few repair calls, paid him at the end of the day, and invited him to come back. Each day, Dad would show up and make whatever repair calls were scheduled for that particular day. He was paid each week for the hours of work he accumulated. It wasn't the most secure employment. I am sure that it was some sort of worry for Dad.

Fortunately, as a young boy, I was quite unaware of any of those kinds of concerns. I had no idea of where we fit into this new world of ours. I was preoccupied with the things that a little boy could be interested in and didn't know for the moment how some others might view our status and station. Fairly quickly, I was able to make friends with some boys who lived across the road, and the adjustment to my new surroundings went well … at first.

But then, the new school year began, and I found myself trying to make new friends, as I was immersed in a somewhat different cultural environment. Coming home from school one day, my mom noticed something just wasn't quite right. In reply to her questioning me about what might be the problem, I responded that some of the kids at school were telling me that I talked funny.

If I was expecting some sympathy or some correcting comment from my mom castigating my accusers, I was to be sadly disappointed. She simply said, "Well, son, you do talk funny." What does a seven-year-old do with that? The reality was that, coming from the hills of Kentucky, we didn't talk like those folks. We were different, and we too had a name that had been given to us. Actually, there were several, the kindest of which was "hillbillies."

Some time ago, I enjoyed being introduced to a TV series that focused on the story of the life of Jesus Christ. I found that the script of *The Chosen* stayed very much in line with what is found in the New Testament. However, it was written in a way that revealed more about how the real-life interaction and conversations may have actually taken place between Christ and those who had close contact with him.

In one of the early episodes, the storyline moved along with Jesus calling some of his early disciples to come and follow him. Some of those early invitations went forth to simple fishermen, with Jesus telling them to drop their nets and he would make them fishers of men. Faith derived from some of the early miracles performed prompted some of the early disciples to act on that invitation.

In the production's retelling of how the relationships between Christ and his chosen disciples evolved, there came moments when the disciples began to form doubts about some of Jesus' associations with others. They witnessed him freely mingling with people of Samaria, publicans, prostitutes and lepers, all of whom were treated as outcasts in the Jewish community at that time. Seeing some questioning his actions, and hearing some murmuring, Jesus tells his disciples that if they are going to follow him, they will need to change. His specific instruction for them at that moment was, "If you are going to follow me, get used to 'different.'"

I like the thought that this could have been one of those interactions that took place between Jesus and his followers, as he was trying to bring about significant change through the message he was sharing. The storyline of that show reminded me of an experience I had a few years back.

My career in country club management had taken me back to reside in Kentucky for the first time since my childhood. One day I was having some conversation with one of my members. She and her daughter were having lunch, and I had stopped by their table to say hello. During our brief chat, I discovered that the daughter and her husband had moved back to my hometown in the hills of Eastern Kentucky.

I inquired as to their experience relative to any adjustments that may have come with the move. She shared that it had taken some time, but after two years, they had made some friends and were finally feeling more comfortable. She related that recently her neighbor had let her know that she and her husband were now considered "brought-ons." That is how the locals casually referred to outsiders who had made it through the process of being accepted into the community.

The sharing of her story reminded me of those early experiences of mine when I was learning about how we are all treated as "different" in one way or another. As I have reflected on that and many other experiences of life, it seems to me that we are all constantly going through the process of bringing others on and being "brought on" ourselves. The gift of the unique attributes and background that we each possess sometimes makes acceptance of one another a challenge. The "bringing-on" process isn't always an easy one. Perhaps the walking of that path and learning to be accepting of our differences is just another piece of the purpose of this existence.

The world becomes a better place when we can all feel like we have been "brought on." That comes for others when we experience one of the most undervalued opportunities and lessons of this life. That being the growth process for each one of us as we learn to become more tolerant, understanding, accepting and appreciative of others—those who are less like us in one way or another.

The table conversation with my member and her daughter that afternoon was another reminder that whether we are the ones being brought or the ones doing the bringing, it is all a part of the good thing that can happen when we discover the better way … the path that takes us to that "get used to different" place in our lives.

8-B and the First Epiphany

I CLEARLY REMEMBER THE moment of my first epiphany.

There may have been some earlier moment of awakening, but there was no denying that this one was the real deal. It came to me near the end of my eighth grade school year.

My classmates and I were in the process of going through a round of sit-down sessions with our guidance counselor. We were receiving counsel on how our particular aptitude and interests might match up with various curriculum options.

The conversations with my classmates outside those counseling sessions was a discussion of another kind.

Much of the focus of those conversations revolved around the question of what career path we might choose that would allow us to make a good living, without working ourselves to death.

If I had had a working knowledge of algebra at that point, I could have used an equation to illustrate what some of us were seeing as the end game. The formula would have been something like $X + Y = Z$, with X being "the least amount of effort" and Y being "the most amount of money." Of course, Z would have equaled "the ideal career." You have to remember, after all, we were just young, immature fourteen-year-olds. My math teachers would have later been able to attest that math probably wasn't my best subject, but this was one algebraic formula that I had down.

The eighth grade had been a real challenge for me. In those days, there was no middle school. You just jumped from grade school, with playground recess, to high school, sitting with juniors and seniors in study hall. The many adjustments began with our arrival on the very first day of school as we learned of our homeroom assignments.

I found myself in 8-B. Among the twenty-some students in that homeroom were several who had been former grade school classmates. By the end of that first day, we all had figured out a few things. For one, we discovered that there were five homeroom groups that had absorbed all the kids coming up from the four elementary schools. Each of them were identified with an alphabetical and numerical combination label: 8-A, 8-B, 8-C, 8-D and 8-E.

The other thing that we were able to sort out that first day was that each of us had been given our homeroom assignments based in some way on our academic performance in grade school. The kids considered to be the best students were to be found in 8-A. Those with the poorest performance made up the 8-E roster.

I am ashamed to admit that, at that moment, I was little concerned about all my fellow students. I was focused on my favorite subject, me, and being disappointed in not finding myself in the 8-A group. But, deep down, I knew I had earned my pay. Heretofore, I had excelled in only one subject, the discipline of avoiding good study habits. I was reaping what I had sown. My study work ethic at that point in my life really should have earned me an assignment in 8-E.

But I consoled myself with the thought that 8-B was still considered "above average," and so I did little that school year to improve my study habits. I earned satisfactory grades in English and history. But it was only the "fear for my life" feeling that Mr. Elinger, our assistant football coach-turned-science teacher, brought to the classroom that allowed me to barely pass that class with a "D" grade. Unfortunately for me, Mr. Simmons, my eighth grade math teacher, wasn't a football coach. I flunked math.

So, it was that at the end of the school year that I found myself sitting with my parents in the superintendent's office, discussing whether I should be moved on to the ninth grade. Ultimately, the decision was left to me. At that moment, I knew two things for sure. I knew that I was capable of doing the work to earn the better grades. I also knew that I didn't want to be labeled a loser.

It was only days later, with these things fresh in my mind, when the epiphanous moment overtook me. It came as if a light switch in my brain had suddenly been tripped that replaced the darkness with the light. The revelation came as I was walking down the hallway between classes. I remember the exact place and the moment. It wasn't like a bolt of lightning, more an awareness accompanied by a feeling of peace.

I suddenly understood that it mattered less what career path I chose to pursue, whether it be teacher, doctor, accountant, farmer or any other profession. The piece of paper that I would be given to hang on the wall would be meaningless if, in the educational process, I didn't learn how to produce. I could correct my study habits, improve my grades and be promoted on to the next grade each year, and I could eventually earn some sort of diploma that certified me to be knowledge-able about something. But that would not be enough. I knew that there had to be something more that came in the process.

I often reflect on that eighth grade year. I wonder how many of my classmates allowed their home-room assignment to determine the limits of their life's potential. I would like to think that no matter the label, most of them found their way to having a productive and fulfilling life. But there is a sadness deep inside because I know that for some, that may not be the case.

For me, as I entered the ninth grade the following fall, I not only knew that an "8-B" performance would not be good enough, I also knew that just being an "8-A" performer might not cut it either. My education had to be more than just showing up and passing tests. The lesson of that first epiphany had taught me that life was more than just moving from one grade to the next. I had to learn how to become a useful and productive member of society.

Somehow, I had to learn how to make things happen.

Up a Snowy Creek

As I CONTINUED TO move through my high school years, I did make some progress toward becoming someone with purpose. My teachers and mentors who were beginning to touch my life would occasionally share some emphasis on the need for planning and developing goals. For me, the need was obvious, but understanding the mechanics of a productive process that could make the concept meaningful would end up taking years.

I found that the words of one of the axioms repeatedly shared with me, "If you fail to plan … you plan to fail," rang true. But understanding the real meaning beyond those words took more than just hearing them repeated. Unfortunately, I am one of those visual learners who often needs the lesson driven home in living color.

It was a cold winter day in the middle of my high school years when one of those colorful, needed lessons was delivered. In a quite unexpected way, I learned that the first run at the planning process isn't always enough. A well-thought-out backup plan is not a bad thing to have, as things don't always work out as expected. Sometimes things can go bad … and sometimes they can go really bad.

Growing up in central Ohio, we always seemed to end up with our fair share of snowfall in the winter months. My friends and I had several good spots for sledding. My favorite was a steep hill that my best friend and I would frequently use. During our various adventures together, Greg broke his arm twice, with both of those incidents occurring when there was plenty of snow on the ground.

The first came in the middle of a good snowstorm, when we decided that it would be a good day for a game of touch football. We had watched the Green Bay Packers slug it out on Lambeau Field and the Cleveland Browns play in the swirling snow of Lakefront Stadium on the shore of Lake Erie. We thought our version of that, played with some of our small-town neighborhood younger boys, would be a lot of fun. There is just something about playing a football game with kids who are several years younger than you that makes you feel like an NFL hall-of-famer. Our "stadium" was the empty lot behind Greg's folks' country store. The snow looked soft, and we thought we were pretty tough, but the ground was frozen and hard as a rock … and Greg ended up with his arm in a plaster cast for six weeks.

The second break of that same arm came with us having a different kind of fun … snow-sledding on that favorite hill of ours.

It was a steep hill, with a downhill slope of about seventy-five yards. The track was just long enough to make for a really good run but not too long that you would mind the climb back up after the fun ride down. The only bad thing was that at the bottom of that hill was a shallow creek that allowed the drainage from rain and snow to meander easily down through the valley. You would have about twenty yards of flat ground at the bottom of the hill before you would come upon that creek. A narrow steel-pipe culvert had been placed there to allow for small equipment and foot traffic, with the crossing measuring about eight feet in width.

When that hill was covered with a foot or more of snow, it would take us a few runs to pack the snow down so that a good sledding course was formed. There are not many things that have the potential for more thrills than a well-prepared snow track on a steep hill in the middle of winter. However, when the thrill of the moment is in front of you, there is a tendency to give less thought to any possible hazardous consequences. Another hard lesson was just around the corner for my friend and me.

It was one memorable Christmas morning that Greg found, among his presents under the tree, a seven-foot wooden toboggan. We eagerly awaited the first good snow and headed off to find out how that new sled would handle that hill of ours. A toboggan is truly a thing of beauty and will pick up some good speed going down a well-formed track. As we went about sizing up our sledding tactics for the day, with just a little thought, we quickly devised a plan. In the event of a run not going well, we figured we could always bail out before coming to that culvert crossing at the bottom of the hill. We were keeping our options simple and uncomplicated. What could possibly go wrong?

Things went well the first few runs as we worked at carving out the sledding trail. Even with the track only partially formed, we found that the toboggan was much faster than any sled we had taken down that hill. As the afternoon wore on, the snow on the trail began to pack and harden. The slightly warming temperatures allowed for a thaw and a refreezing of the surface. Preoccupied with the thrill of enjoying one good run after another, we hardly noticed that our sledding track was gradually becoming more a sheet of ice than a hillside of soft, newly fallen snow.

I can't remember how many of those runs we made before the inevitable happened. We found ourselves picking up too much speed and as we began losing control, with our sled moving off the track, I bailed. The first part of our plan worked out well, as I safely rolled away from our runaway toboggan. Greg wasn't so lucky, barely being able to push himself off just before he hit the creek. Unfortunately, at the last moment as he slid his body away from the runaway toboggan, his arm found a piece of iron pipe that ran alongside the edge of the creek.

Greg and I had taken time to make plans for a fun day of sledding, but we hadn't taken time to come up with a "plan B" that would allow us to deal with the unexpected. It's always good to have a good plan B. My friend trudged home with a broken arm … with me following, dragging a splintered sled. Sometimes it's hard being young and dumb … and sometimes one finds life moving along just as fast as a sled on a long, steep icy hill.

That's when, if you aren't careful, you might find yourself lying up some cold, snowy creek, with a broken arm and sled, instead of just being … short the proverbial paddle.

Seventeen

THERE ARE TIMES WHEN a parent would choose to take their child's place and not have them suffer through a difficult experience. The same can be said of a child who would do the same for their loving father or mother. Perhaps it is best that we each experience our own share of the pain and joy that comes to us in this life. In any event, that is never a choice that is available to us. We share all of whatever comes, in the time and way that it is given.

My mom was only five years old when she lost her mother. Hemorrhaging, following the birth of Mom's youngest sister, took her life. She was only thirty years old. Her husband was left to raise seven girls.

It was a little over a year later that Mom's father remarried a widow who had four children of her own. They later had a child together, which made for an even dozen growing up under one roof.

I have always thought, economic challenges aside, that once you have two children, you may as well have a dozen. A first child changes everything for a couple, but once that second child arrives, the sorting out of who did what to whom presents another kind of challenge. Actually, the larger family provides more eyewitnesses to any alleged misdeeds that may occur. So, for parenting purposes, a large family does have its advantages. Fortunately, my grandfather was a mining engineer, with steady employment, and was able to provide well for his new wife and large expanding family. But all was not well.

My mother's new stepmother had a jealous side, and truth be told, not everyone has a gift for loving a child who is not their own … let alone seven. Unfortunately for my mother and her sisters, their new mother didn't possess that gift. In turn, each of the girls left home as soon as they possibly could. Mom chose to leave as she was approaching her senior year of high school, taking up residence with an older sister.

She was just seventeen.

As I recall, my mother never spoke much about her childhood. Some understanding of the challenges of her early years first came to me as I would overhear her reminiscing with her sisters. There were always mixed emotions present when they would speak of their "Daddy." I could sense that a special bond had developed between the sisters because of their childhood experiences.

However, Mom never wore any of the pain of those early years on her sleeve. Only those closest to her had any idea regarding the missing pieces of her childhood puzzle. Other than Mom's high school graduation picture, the only other picture we have of her was an early grade school photo. The image in that photo is of a young, innocent girl, seemingly living a happy childhood. But not every picture tells the story. Remaining hidden were the hurts, pain and a void that was never filled after the loss of her mother.

For my siblings and me, as we were children growing up, the long-term effect was that we had a mother who cared for us in a special way. She was quite selfless and loved her children nearly to a fault. Later, in my adult years, I found myself having to occasionally remind her that none of her children, especially me, were perfect. But her love for us was. She was continually finding and reinforcing the good she found in each of us.

There were two things I recall her expressing from time to time. One was her desire for us to stay close to the understanding we had been given of the Gospel. The second was that the only thing she really wanted for herself was to be able to see her children raised to adulthood. This was further proof that she never got over not having a loving mother in her childhood.

For my siblings and me, having both a mom and a dad was a blessing. Growing up, we never had everything we wanted as children. That turned out to be a good thing. But we always had what we needed. I have heard it said that the definition of greed is to want more than you need. Our parents helped teach us the difference between the wants and the needs. Dad would often say that he wouldn't raise us any different, even if he had a million dollars. That was in a time when a million dollars was a real fortune. The other thing I recall him sharing with us was the thought that there will always be those who have more than us, and there will always be those who have less ... just be sure to be grateful for what you have.

But what we didn't have in "things" was more than made up for in love, and it was given to us in various ways.

One of those ways was the giving of a little special attention on our birthdays. We could always count on Mom making our favorite cake to mark our special day. My birthday cake preference as a child was simply a white cake with vanilla icing. You have heard it said that sometimes you can have your cake and eat it too. The birthday I remember best may have been the one where that didn't happen for me.

The day of my seventeenth birthday was much like any other day. As I came home from school, I found Mom sitting in the family room, folding some laundry. I walked through the room and shared the thought that today was certainly a special day. I have always been one to share my thoughts, and the sharing of this one was my way of teasingly reminding my mom of her son's birthday. It was completely unnecessary for me to provide that reminder, as I knew that Mom never forgot any of our birthdays. However, I found some satisfaction in her confirming for me that my day was indeed a very special day.

I followed the passing interaction with an inquiry as to whether there might be a cake made to celebrate the occasion. Another unnecessary question, just a little more of the teasing we both enjoyed. Mom let me know that my cake could be found on the kitchen counter. I immediately proceeded into the kitchen, and sure enough, there on the counter was the anticipated beautiful double-layered vanilla icing cake.

However, as I drew nearer, things didn't appear quite right. Upon closer inspection, it was clear that the icing was not the usual plain vanilla icing that I loved. For my seventeenth birthday, Mom had made my traditional favorite white cake but had added a healthy blending of coconut shavings in the vanilla icing. This posed a problem for me. At that time in my young life, any thought of using coconut as an ingredient in anything would have been an excellent way to ruin it.

I walked slowly back to the family room and made a hopeful inquiry to my mother: "Is the cake on the kitchen counter my birthday cake?" I was disappointed to hear her respond in the affirmative. I proceeded to share with her that it appeared that the icing on that cake was laced with coconut. To my dismay, she confirmed that indeed it was. Before giving any further thought to the matter, and with no hesitation, I blurted out, "Mom … I hate coconut."

There are two things a person would need to understand about my mother. First of all, she was completely honest and without any trace of guile. Second, she was a person who enjoyed doing things for those she loved. So, the next words that came out of her mouth should not have been completely unexpected. She quickly responded, without any thought or hesitation, "Well, son, your dad loves coconut." My first thought in that moment, for which I am forever grateful I did not share, was, *Well, does this mean for Dad's birthday we will be enjoying a white cake with white vanilla icing?*

With just a bit of reflection, I realized that Mom had no recollection of my distaste for coconut. She just knew Dad loved coconut and thought I would too. Mom's innocent, honest response was a lesson for me. As I reflected on it, I was reminded that she was always doing for others and never expected anything in return. She had an honest, loving, serving nature; it was one of her greatest strengths.

Over the years, I would on occasion enjoy the retelling of that story, usually around my birthday, and revisit with Mom one of our most enjoyable shared moments. We would always have a good laugh together, as I would playfully tease her about how her poor little son's birthday was ruined because of a few flakes of coconut.

So, I have little recollection of the birthday gifts I received in my growing-up years. But I have never forgotten the special gift I received the day I turned seventeen…that gift being how a moment of disappointment opened a bit wider the door to a better understanding and appreciation of my mom. How different each of our seventeenth birthdays must have been.

In retrospect, I guess I must admit that the day I turned seventeen, I did get to have my cake … and eat it, too. I wouldn't trade the memory of that seventeenth birthday coconut-laced vanilla icing cake for anything.

The irony in it all is that as an adult, I love everything coconut … even when it is sprinkled on vanilla icing cakes.

Late in life, my mom's father suffered a debilitating heart attack. Following some rehabilitation, he was released into our family's care. Though he had to move around with the aid of a cane, his mind was sharp.

We lived next to a country store, and on some of the hottest days of summer, he would ask if I would go to the store and get an ice cream treat for him. I remember on one occasion, I asked him specifically what he would like me to get for him. He hesitated a moment and then reflected, "Those ice cream sandwiches are ten cents … and the sherbet push-ups are seven cents. I believe the push-ups are the better value." It wasn't that he did not have sufficient money in his bank account. It was just that habits carried over from the Great Depression never left him.

Papaw lived with us for the remaining months of his life. Every day, Mom provided loving care for her father, seeing that his every personal need was attended to. There were moments during that time for conversation between just father and daughter.

Years later, I learned of a poignant moment shared between the two. They were speaking of the times after the loss of a wife and mother and how things had changed afterward. In an honest moment of sharing, Mom related that a hurtful difference had been made in how the children of the household were treated. She shared some feelings regarding the lack of a loving mother in her childhood years … and a father who did little to fill that gap.

That conversation ended with my mother asking a question of her father. It was one she had probably given much thought to over the years since her childhood. Searching for some answer that had yet to be found, she asked, "Daddy, why did you allow my sisters and me to be treated the way we were … with a stepmother who did so much for her children and so little for us?" After a moment of reflection, he shared, "Well, her children didn't have a father." My mother's honest, painful response was, "We didn't have a father … or a mother."

No doubt "seventeen" brought back different kinds of memories for my mom and me. I am grateful for the ones that I have to remember and cherish. For my mom, I only wish that some of hers could have been different.

Part Two
Recognition

Sometimes the light of understanding comes about instantaneously, when we suddenly can see something more clearly that was previously hidden from our view.

The "aha moment."

It may come as you hear a combination of the melody and lyrics of a song that moves your heart and touches your soul. You may sense it in the reading of a passage, the hearing of a meaningful quote or as you watch an unforgettable line being delivered in a scene on the big screen. The instant you experience that moment, it touches you in a special way. You get it.

Other times, the unveiling may be years in the making. That often comes about as several separate events or experiences conspire to bring about a revelation that opens up your understanding and has meaning for you. When that happens, it can be like the closing line in a play, where everything seems to come together and make sense. No matter how it may come … at that moment, you get it.

Whether the recognition comes in the moment or with the passage of time, it is the opening of another door that allows you to continue your journey toward a better understanding of what this life is all about. It becomes the discovery of just another missing piece of the puzzle.

You Really Can't Judge That Book

SOME OF OUR BEST memories are those originating around past holidays, especially the Christmas season. The following is an unusual one that came to me later in life. I wish I would have had the benefit of the experience when I was younger, but we can't choose when or how memories are made. They just happen.

Once again, the Christmas season was upon us, so it was the time for the sending and receiving of gifts.

Therefore, it was not entirely unexpected when a package arrived in the mail just a few days before Christmas. It was addressed to me and was obviously a book. There was no card inserted within which would provide a clue for who the sender might be.

The cover on the book read: *Edward Van Halen: A Definitive Biography.*

I immediately made a note to myself that it was not *the* definitive biography … just *a* definitive biography. Upon perusing the outer jacket of the book, I discovered that the author was just a huge fan of Eddie Van Halen, who felt inspired to write a story of his life … and what it meant to him.

So, the question was, who gifted me this book? There were the usual suspects. My children knew I loved to read and had given me books in the past. My siblings have always shared an enjoyment of many things rock 'n' roll. It's possible that one of them may have thought I might enjoy a book that they had found to be an enjoyable read. Perhaps the present was a gift from our neighbor Elaine. We had recently invited her to come with us and experience an Alice Cooper concert. Perhaps joining us in meeting the man himself was the inspiration for the giving.

But why a book about Eddie Van Halen?

Though I had enjoyed some Van Halen songs over the years, I don't think I'd ever mentioned to anyone a particular thought about Eddie Van Halen's band or their music. I had a brief, tempting thought that I should just return the book to Barnes & Noble and exchange it for another title. But then the thought came to me that someone chose this book for me. A gift should be appreciated.

And so it was on Christmas Eve, with all of my preparations for the holidays completed, I found myself beginning my journey of reading a story about the life of Edward Van Halen ... or so I thought.

As I read the first few lines of the first chapter, the style struck me as most unusual. The author was using a first-person speaking voice in describing a horrific crime that he had become a part of. I thought, *How original*, and wondered how this was going to ultimately tie into the Van Halen biography described in brief on the outer cover. It was an interesting lead-in and, despite the overly descriptive inclusion of minute details that seemingly could take me nowhere, I found myself anxiously turning the pages.

As I plunged on into the second chapter, I anticipated finding a change in the storyline that would smartly move me to the ultimate subject of the book.

I was surprised to find a read that closely resembled more a traditional mystery novel than a fan's reflections on the life of a celebrity idol. I found it not just unusual but very strange.

A part of my Christmas mystery was solved as I removed the outer cover of the *Edward Van Halen: A Definitive Biography* and realized that I was actually holding in my hands a copy of the novel *Memory Man* by David Baldacci. Somewhere, along the line, a publishing company employee had failed to match up the book with the appropriate cover.

So now, the question became, who knew that I loved everything written by David Baldacci? Sounds like a good first line for a best-selling mystery novel. Once again, I was reminded of the old adage, you just can't judge a book by its cover.

The first impression is always important, but it's what you find inside that really counts, both in books and people. As the journey of my life moved through my formative years of youth and on into adulthood, I was to find that lesson being driven home, over and over again.

Mornings with Bill

I OFTEN THINK OF an old friend whom I have not seen for a number of years now ... actually, more years than I would like to admit. I don't remember exactly the first time I made Bill's acquaintance. I guess it really isn't important. But I will never forget the first time he made a significant impression on me.

I had taken a job as a controller in a private country club. I had wrestled with that decision a bit. My upbringing and early life experiences were just about as far away as you could get from life around the country club setting. But in the end, I decided that the position would be a nice addition to my resume and career experience. I could sense that the club's general manager, who offered me the position, would be someone I could enjoy working with. He had made a comment in our final interview that I thought curious, but one that turned out to be prophetic. Encouraging me to consider his offer, he remarked that it just might be a career-changing opportunity.

My read on enjoying working with the GM turned out to be spot-on. We got along well, and I began accumulating some valuable experience in an environment that was completely new to me. As we reviewed the financial statements each month, he would point out the line items that were most critical, and I quickly began to sort out the financial side of the club business. I had found another in a long line of mentors who was helping me in the broadening of my experience. Little did I know that our association was destined to be a short one.

As the newness of the position began to wear off and I become more acclimated to my new surroundings, some unexpected pieces of a picture began to come into focus. An impression was forming that the circle of those who could get along with and like my boss was not what I would have thought it ought to be.

The truth is, it can be lonely at the top. There were those who had developed differences with the club's GM, and some of those were individuals in positions of influence. As I became more aware of the concerns, I found myself stuck in the middle. I struggled somewhat to understand why it was that he and I could get along so well, when so many problems were developing with others.

And then, one day, I remember Bill walking into the club business office. He served on the club's House Committee and had stopped in to ask our receptionist, Sandy, if she could make a few copies for him. He had found some articles about the restaurant business that he thought he would share at that evening's committee meeting.

The request had no sooner been voiced than my boss stepped out of his office and, in a somewhat confrontational manner, instructed Sandy to charge Mr. Bratton ten cents for each of those copies. Witnessing that interaction, I knew I would probably not be working with my boss too much longer. And, sure enough, it was not too many days later that the club's general manager was relieved of his duties, and I was asked to function as the interim manager. The career change comment did indeed turn prophetic, and that change began a club management career for me that was to span four decades.

As I assumed my management duties at the club, I found Bill stopping by the club business office nearly every morning. He lived just around the corner and would come by, get a cup of coffee, and check in with the office staff. He would usually look in on me and see how I was doing. Most mornings it was just a quick hello. But occasionally, I would find myself having a long conversation discussing some aspect of club operations with Bill. There were times when those sessions might last an hour or longer.

Bill was never shy about sharing his opinions with me. In the book *The Last 100 Days* by John Toland, the author quotes Clement Attlee as always remembering a comment about Churchill: "There's Winston; he has half a dozen solutions to every problem, and one of them is right, but the trouble is he doesn't know which it is." Bill never had trouble figuring out what the right solution was to any particular problem.

I guess I should tell you just a couple of other things about Bill. Like everyone else in this world whom I have come to know, including myself, he had his share of imperfections. I am not sure how many real friends Bill had at the club. Standing just an inch or two over five feet, he made up for his lack of height by being very direct in his approach to sharing his opinions. He had a little bit of the Napoleon complex in him. Well, truth be told, maybe more than a little bit.

It was rumored that he had been a good salesman and had become a partner in a successful business, but eventually his partners paid him a significant sum of money not to have to put up with him—and his opinions—anymore. I am not sure about all of that, but I know that Bill would have admitted to being quite the character. I think it would be fair to say that Bill had strong opinions on a lot of things, and most people probably had a strong opinion about Bill. But that can be said of a lot of folks.

In club folklore, it was reputed that on one occasion, Bill had approached a foursome having lunch in the men's grill. It was observed that as he went about the usual sharing of his views, those at the table were apparently not in agreement with Bill's perspective on the matter being discussed. As the conversation became more heated, one of the men took his beverage and poured it into Bill's sports coat pocket. Not everyone was blessed with enough patience to endure some of Bill's dialogues.

For some reason, Bill took a liking to me. On one of his first early morning visits, he gave me a copy of the Dale Carnegie book *How to Win Friends and Influence People*. Though his visits often took more of my time than I would sometimes really have, I knew he was trying to help me become a good manager. In those morning sessions with Bill, I learned one of the most important lessons in business: always be respectful and willing to listen to what the other person has to say.

During my time and association with Bill, our conversations would usually gravitate around club operations. As was his nature, he would often share specific suggestions on how he thought improvements could be implemented. I would often find his "suggestions" helpful. But I also had to give less attention to some of his "best solutions," as we would discuss issues relating to member service and programs. To his credit, he always accepted my judgment on any of those issues we discussed. I am not sure that he allowed that latitude in all of his relationships.

I didn't have a long association with Bill before I headed on to my next opportunity. It was just six months following my departure that I received the news that Bill had passed away. But I never forgot the time we had together in those morning sessions. My good friend and mentor, Bill Bratton, would be pleased to know that I took many of the lessons shared in the book he gave me to heart.

In the reading of Carnegie's book and from my morning conversations with Bill, I developed a philosophical approach to life that would serve me well. I came to summarize and share it in the following way with many of my associates over the years: "If you want to be successful, find out what a person wants, and find a way to give it to them."

There was another takeaway from those early morning sessions with Bill. On one of the last of his early morning visits, he shared with me one of his "best solution" suggestions. By my response, he could sense that I was giving little consideration to his arguments for the taking of a specific action. Near the end of our conversation, following a thoughtful pause, Bill took a moment to tactfully remind me that even a broken clock is right twice a day and that I probably should not be so quick to discount the opinions of others.

The moments spent with Bill helped me understand the importance of keeping an open mind and being willing to listen to the viewpoints of others … that something can be learned from everyone.

I try to remember that lesson every time someone interrupts an enjoyable lunch, leaving me tempted to pour my favorite beverage into their coat pocket.

Playing with a Stacked Deck

THE THREE OF US paused, withholding any conversation, as the next hand was dealt. I was hoping my luck would turn, sooner rather than later. What I thought was going to be just an evening of a little fun and entertainment was turning into something I hadn't counted on.

I was on a losing streak, and I was looking for just one hand to salvage the night. That is what a big-time gambler does, right? You delude yourself into thinking that it can be the next deal that will pull you out from all the accumulated losses.

How was it that I seemed to be continually grasping defeat out of the jaws of victory? Deal after deal, I was coming so close to taking the house, only to end up seeing what I thought was a sweet hand suddenly turn sour.

The memory was of a night from long ago, when I had my first lesson that you can't win when you are playing with a marked, or a stacked, deck.

I have heard of some of the tricks that can happen in Vegas. Loaded dice and rules of the games stack the odds against you ever having a chance to walk away the winner. I know that in the long run, you can never beat the house. Years ago, I had a client who sold his business, packed up and headed out west to work the tables. What is it about the lure of the game that, like a magnet, pulls people in? I occasionally wonder how that move turned out for my friend. Was it the pot of gold at the end of the rainbow he was hoping it would be … or just a loser's draw?

When you think about it, a lot of things in life are a bit of a gamble. I reflect on how I have had my share of wins and losses. Over time, one of the things I have learned is that your best bet is in holding the right cards at the right time … and knowing how and when to play them.

I love the culture of the network marketing world. Some folks think of the multi-level marketing arena as just another version of Vegas, pyramid schemes with some of the players ending up holding nothing but a losing hand. But in any business venture you pursue, there is an element of risk, and success is always dependent on building a team of leaders who have the drive to get it done.

One of the mentors I came across in the network marketing world compared the pool of people you come across in life to a deck of cards. Herb was an exceptionally successful leader who had learned to sort out some of the cards you needed to have for a winning hand. He knew that not everyone was ready and capable of being the right fit for his team. In his process of evaluating and sorting out potential leaders, one of his mantras was, "Some will, some won't … so what." He knew that not everyone could be "all-in" relative to the needed commitment and could be ruthless in discarding from his circle those he felt would be unproductive, or a negative influence.

He promoted the thought that, in the building of your circle of influence—as one plays the hand of life—one of the most important things is the need to understand the cards you are holding. He had developed a way of thinking of the pool of people you come across in this world as playing cards, with each card in the deck possessing characteristics that somewhat defined how they might act and the potential they had to function in a positive way.

In his game, the lower playing cards—the twos, threes, fours and so on had traits that tended to be less positive, the kind that would routinely block the pathways to success. Each successive higher card in the deck had progressively more positive traits that allowed for the possibility to have increased productivity and effective interaction with others. What you were really looking for in building your team were the face cards. The problem is that people aren't cards. The challenge is to figure out whether the card you have just drawn—the person you have brought on your team—is another two who can't help you, or the ace you have been looking for, who will complete your team's winning hand.

Various facets of life can be compared to a card game. There are sometimes things you can control. Other times, you just have to play the hand you are dealt. As much as possible, you want to stack the deck in your favor and not leave success or failure to Lady Luck.

I was counting on a little luck in a final hand that was played so long ago, but the reality was that luck could play no part in the hands the dealer was passing out that evening. Though I didn't realize it at the time, I had absolutely no chance to come away a winner. The fix was on.

Fortunately for me, I wasn't at one of the tables in Vegas, with my business or life's savings on the line as a final wager at risk on the last hand. I was playing a game of Old Maid with my two youngest daughters, and they had been killing me all night. I was losing the game to two little girls, ages four and seven. How was it that one of them was managing to win every single hand? The fun evening had become very one-sided, with all the fun stacking up with their pile of chips.

That last hand ended up being just like all the rest. One of those girls was the winner, and my losing streak remained intact. It was shortly after that that I came to understand that the girls' continual giggling throughout the evening had nothing to do with the winning of hands but the playing of tricks. I had written off all those giggling moments as little girls being a little giddy, enjoying some fun moments with their dad. But there was something more sinister at work in that evening's game of Old Maid. The con had been on all evening long.

As they gathered up all their chips, my seven-year-old daughter handed me the old maid card and showed me how she had carefully clipped a very small, almost imperceptible, piece off the top of the card. All evening long, they had known in whose hand the old maid was residing, never failing to take unfair advantage of me, hand after hand. What father would have thought that his young girls were on the path of becoming card sharks? Those little waifs had figured out, at a very young age, that playing with a marked deck always has its advantages.

It was later in life that I was to learn some of the card-playing lessons of the business world, one of those being the tactic of stacking one's deck for success. But for me, that night's game was another kind of lesson … that though you can't stack the deck of life, you can choose to not let the other "dealers" around the table set the house rules or control the game.

And if you are ever playing a friendly game of Old Maid with your daughters, my best advice would be to bring your own deck of cards to the gaming table.

Everything that happens in Vegas ... should stay in Vegas.

Right Place … Wrong Time

PATIENCE—WHO AMONG US has enough of it? We live in a culture where we want everything, and we want it now.

I have always enjoyed good comedy. As the saying goes, laughter is the best medicine. What's the difference between a good comedian and a great one? Good material is important, but delivery is critical … and timing may be the most crucial element of the delivery in the routine. The really great ones have a sense, and the patience that goes with it, that allows for the appropriate pause and the killer punchline.

One of the most enjoyable experiences of my youth was my time playing Little League baseball. It was my first sport. Outside the family circle, it was the first place that I was able to develop self-confidence.

I would hit and catch with some of my friends in the neighborhood. I spent hours bouncing a tennis ball off the garage door, throwing harder and harder as I developed my reflexes. Eventually, even with my hardest throws, the ball couldn't get past me. It took a lot of throws to get to that point.

I also seemed to have a knack for getting my bat on the ball. My hand-eye coordination allowed me to rarely strike out. Though I was small, with never a thought of trying to drive a ball over the outfield fence, I hit for a good average, and I loved to run the bases. My Little League coach was my first non-family mentor. He taught us boys the fundamentals of the game and continuously gave us positive encouragement as we improved our playing skills.

We had four levels of play in our community's youth baseball organization. Eight-year-olds started out in the Bantam League, and as your skills developed, each year's spring tryouts determined when your playing level could allow you to move up to the Minors, then Majors, and finally Babe Ruth.

My first two years in the Bantam League were years of learning and progression. When tryouts came around the following spring, though I was pretty small, my fielding earned me a tryout to move two levels up to the Majors. I had a really small beginner's ball glove. All the other players trying out for the team had the advantage of better equipment. I was disappointed to be sent down to the Minors in the last cut. But my physical size and maturity were determining factors that could not be ignored. I really didn't have any business playing up in the Majors with those older boys. It was my first lesson in being in the right place, at the wrong time. I really wanted to be there … I just wasn't ready.

I think Mom and Dad felt bad that I came close and missed an opportunity. Dad made sure I had a better glove for my play down in the Minors that season. My fielding improved with the new glove, and my hitting improved even more. But for all of the good plays I was able to make that season, the memory that is the clearest is of one game near the end of the season when I came to the plate with two out and two men in scoring position. It was the bottom of the ninth, and we were one run behind.

After taking a couple of practice swings in the on-deck circle, I stepped up to the plate. As I prepared to move into my batting stance, I glanced back and saw my dad seated in the stands. Dad was my first hitting coach. He threw the first pitch I ever took a swing at. Though we were both right-handed, he taught me to hit from the left side of the plate, just like him. As I prepared to face down the opposing pitcher, it almost felt like Dad was standing in the batter's box with me.

As I turned my attention to the pitcher out on the mound, although I was a bit anxious, I was full of confidence. I wanted to hit that ball through one of the holes in that infield so bad I could taste it. Relaxing my stance just a bit, I took a couple more abbreviated practice swings, using my familiar backhand movement to bring the bat evenly across the plate. All I wanted at that moment was to do what I had done so many times before: just get a good clean single and drive in those two runs … and show Dad that I had learned well what he had tried to teach me.

But the day was not to be mine. I struck out on three straight pitches. I just wanted it too much. I probably wasn't as patient in waiting for the ball to cross that plate at the exact time that my bat was looking to meet it. Timing.

Great memories, though. I still love the smell of the leather glove and can still remember the feeling when my bat would find the sweet spot as I connected with a good fastball. So, it was many years later that I was excited when my first child interested in playing baseball told me that he wanted to sign up for Little League. Like some parents, I was hopeful my son would enjoy the experience as much as I had. I couldn't wait for league sign-up day to come around.

I had arrived a little earlier than the announced meeting time. As I entered the meeting room space, I noticed a head table and podium in the front of the room. Scattered across the large hall were eight-foot-long tables with the accompanying chairs. I was a bit surprised, as I was expecting a gathering of fifteen or twenty people. It appeared the room was set for one hundred or more.

I was excited to see so many folks interested in a Little League organizational meeting. The other sport leagues my son's older sisters had played in had just a handful of adults helping make everything happen. As I looked around the room, I thought, *This must really be some organization!*

While waiting for the start of the meeting, I had a few minutes to size up the group. I noticed that there was much animated conversation at most of the tables. I didn't recognize anyone in the room, which was a bit unusual. But everyone seemed to be pumped up. I was too. That was always the feeling I would get when spring approached and I would pull my bat and ball glove off the shelf and head off to the ball field.

Upon closer inspection, I noticed some of the guys nearest me were inspecting some fishing lures they had laid out on their table. They seemed to be sharing stories about a recent fishing adventure. Well, I was never much into fishing, but I knew a lot of guys considered it a sport. I just never got excited about sitting in a boat waiting for a fish to bite, and baiting a hook with an earthworm didn't top my list of fun things to be doing either.

It was about that time that a couple of guys sat down at the head table. They wore caps, but they were not what I would have thought of as ones who would fit with a baseball uniform. They had sort of an outdoorsy look to them. In fact, one of the two had some kind of decorative hook and sinker adorning his hat. The look seemed a bit silly to me. I couldn't imagine holding a baseball bat in my hand with that thing on my head.

As one of the men stood and approached the podium, I took one more look around the room. In a room full of prospective baseball coaches, there wasn't one cap in the room with any baseball insignia. Could there be this many guys with not a diehard Yankees, Reds or Dodgers fan among them? Something just wasn't right, and I was about to find out what it was.

I shouldn't have been surprised when the meeting was called to order and I heard the individual at the podium welcoming everyone to the Bass Masters Annual Meeting. My Little League organizational meeting was scheduled for the following Saturday. I was a week early. Once again, I was in the right place ... just at the wrong time.

In the 1960s, a band came on the scene that had a unique sound. It was a time when acoustic folk was transitioning to electric rock, and no one did it quite like The Byrds. Some of their most successful hits combined lyrics of songwriters like Bob Dylan and Pete Seeger with their gift of artful harmonizing. One of their early songs was a tune where Seeger had lifted much of the lyrics right from the Old Testament book of Ecclesiastes. The song was titled "Turn! Turn! Turn!" It's a great song, with a good message: how in life there is a time and a season for everything.

It's been said that patience is a virtue. It's more than that. It can make all the difference. It's all about being in the right place, at the right time ... and doing what you ought to be doing at that moment in time. Whether you are trying to make an audience laugh, have your bat connect with that hard fastball or not end up spending your morning with a bunch of fishing nuts, timing is everything. And good timing is all about developing the necessary patience.

I'm still working on developing enough of that patience stuff to join my buddies for a day at the lake, waiting for some fish to bite. To everything there will be a season.

I have a feeling that one may be a long time coming.

A Rose by Any Other Name

I FIRST MET ROSE on a visit to one of our local department stores, though it was some weeks later before a formal introduction came about. At the time, it seemed as if it were simply a chance encounter. I was to learn it was something much more than that. It's funny how the lesson that is sometimes there to be learned isn't given to us in just one session but unfolds over time.

Years before, after finishing high school, I had continued my education at the local branch of a state university. That enabled me to live at home and keep my education expenses reasonable. Being the oldest of six children, that was a great help for my parents as they worked at managing the family budget. Staying close to home for a couple more years was an enjoyable added benefit.

It was at about that time that our family became acquainted with the executive director of the county children's services. In addition, one of the social workers on staff had also become a good friend of the family. One day, my folks received a completely unexpected phone call. There was a need for a family to take in a newborn infant for a few days. The mother had made arrangements for her child to be adopted, but the required paperwork necessitated an interim arrangement for a short period of time. Children's services felt our home would be an ideal fit to fill that need.

That experience opened a door, and the delivery and short-term stay of that little one was followed by several other temporary additions in our home. About a year later, I left home and was away from the family for two years. Though I would write and receive frequent letters, it was years later that I learned that not everything finds its way into letters from home, and sometimes the omissions can be significant.

Time had slipped by following my return home. I had married, and my wife and I had started a family of our own. It seems a bit of a mystery how your children can grow up so fast. From the moment they are born, each day brings changes, and the days and weeks almost imperceptibly turn into months … and years. Time waits for no one, suddenly you are older, and those babies aren't babies anymore. I think there comes a time in most parents' lives when they reflect and wish those little ones could have stayed little just a little while longer.

Before I knew it, school days came along, and, with them, a new round of learning opportunities. I was pleasantly surprised when my oldest daughter asked me to help with coaching her fifth-grade basketball team. I had always loved the game, and I thought helping as an assistant coach would be an enjoyable experience. I am not sure I was much help, but several years later, her younger sister's team needed a coach, and I got a second chance at the coaching thing. I didn't realize at the time what a learning opportunity that coming year was going to be for me, in more ways than one.

As the season was about to begin, I found myself in a department store looking for a new basketball for the girls to use on the outdoor goal in our driveway. Though there were a variety of balls of different brands, quality and price, it took only a few minutes to find just the right ball to fit our needs. As I was about to walk away and make my purchase, I noticed a young woman who seemed to be in the process of trying to do exactly what I had just done. She seemed confused by the array of choices, so I made some inquiry about what she might be looking for.

She explained that her two oldest daughters had taken up the game and she was looking for a ball so they could practice at home. I suggested a choice that might work best for her, and she seemed to appreciate me having taken a moment to help. I walked away feeling good about providing some small bit of service to a stranger and quickly forgot about the encounter. After all, I had a basketball season to prepare for.

What's the difference between a good coach and a great coach? If you are going to have a chance of being a great coach, it really helps to have some good players. You can't win the race without the horses. As I began to work with my daughter's team, I quickly realized I had some really good horses. I had limited coaching experience, but I had enough to have a feeling that the coming season could be an enjoyable one with my girls winning some games. In fact, with all the talent we had, I felt we had a chance to win all our games.

However, visions of an undefeated season were quickly threatened in the opening minutes of the first game of the season. A fourth-grade team will probably score no more than 15 to 20 points in a game, and in the first minute of our first game, the other team scored twice. We were down 4–0 with only a minute played. It was at that moment, as I called a quick timeout, that I realized the difference between coaching young men and young women.

With a boys' team, in that situation, the guys would have come running over to the timeout huddle with every one of them critiquing each other, in most cases each of them confident that they were not the problem. Just get me the ball, Coach. As my girls approached the bench, I observed that they were acting quite differently. There was no panic or pointing of fingers to possible culprits. In fact, there appeared little concern on any of their faces. They seemed to be completely immersed in discussing how the ribbons and bows in their hair were holding up after a minute of action on the court. At that point, I knew I was in trouble. But it only took a little coaching direction, and the girls got their game on track. From that point on, they controlled the play, and we marched on to a convincing victory. The game was never really in doubt. We just had too much talent.

At the sound of the game-ending buzzer, a feeling of euphoria swept over me. My girls had come from behind and brought me a convincing win in my first game as a girls' basketball coach. The thrill of victory is always a great feeling, and I was feeling it in full measure at that moment ... until I paused to look across the gymnasium floor.

There, on the other side of the court, I found my parents. I knew they were planning on being at the game, and I was eager to catch up to them and have them share what a great game the girls had played ... and what a great job of coaching they had just witnessed. But as I found them in the crowd of families and friends, I suddenly had no desire to hurry over to see them, for standing there in conversation with my parents was the young woman whom I had chanced to help in the department store just a few weeks before. I quickly put two and two together and realized that the team we had just soundly defeated had been her daughters' team! The wonderful feeling of euphoria that I had felt just seconds before instantly dissipated to almost nothing. It was one of those moments when you come to understand how something that feels so good can go so bad … so fast.

I thought I would just wait a few minutes before I wandered over to see the folks. But as the minutes ticked by, the young woman continued to remain engaged in conversation with my parents. What could they possibly be conversing about in such length? The thought occurred to me that perhaps she was upset about the loss that her daughters' team had just experienced and had somehow connected me with my parents. It is these kinds of situations where one's doubts and fears tend to take control.

Finally, I felt I couldn't delay the inevitable any longer and began the long walk across the gymnasium. As I approached the small gathering of the young woman, her daughters and my parents, before I could even offer a greeting, my mother excitedly made an introduction. Motioning toward the young woman who had been fully occupying my parents' attention, she excitedly said, "Bo, this is Rose!" I thought, *Well that's nice, but how did my parents come to know the young woman I helped that day in the department store?*

Before I could consider how that question might be answered, Rose made a startling announcement. With some emotion, she said, "Your mom and dad saved my life." It was then that the story was revealed of how Rose had been a troubled youth, having had a life of continually being moved from one foster family to another. It was during that time while I was away for those two years that Rose had come to spend some time with my family. She related how my parents had, in a firm but loving way, provided some needed structure and discipline, and changed her life.

I would leave it to you to decide if my brief encounter with Rose in the department store that day was just a coincidence. Do the things that happen to us in life happen with purpose, or are they just accidental happenstance?

My girls went on to have an undefeated season that year. It had nothing to do with the coach. There was just too much talent on that team. Several of those girls would play ball into their high school years. If you want to win the game, you have to have the horses. We had the horses that year.

Rose's girls' team also had some good players, and they had a good season … finishing in second place, right behind us. But years later, the memory of the wins in that season have less to do with the game scores and more to do with the moment of meeting and helping a stranger in a department store … who turned out to be no stranger at all.

The Big Oak Tree

THERE WERE TIMES IN my club management career when I had a phone line in my office that was a personal direct line. I could always have that line open for my outgoing calls, and my wife had that number when she needed to reach out to me. She was always sensitive about bothering me at work and would only call if it was something of a somewhat serious nature. I always thought of that phone line as the Bat Phone, as in the direct line that the fictional comic character Commissioner Gordon would use to reach Batman when trouble was threatening.

In those days, my desktop phone had five lines, with buttons that would flash when a call was ringing in. There would always be just a bit of a rise in anxiety when I would see my Bat Phone line lighting up, as I would wonder what crisis had developed.

Early one afternoon, as I was sitting working at my desk, the phone rang, and the flashing light indicated that Batman was needed. Following a moment's hesitation, steeling myself to deal with the challenge, with a bit of trepidation, I picked up the receiver. Without any introduction, the message was brief and to the point: "When you get home … we need to talk." Click.

The tone in my wife's voice confirmed that, as with the call that we had just shared, the coming "talk" might not be much of a two-way conversation. It is amazing how a short call like that can be disconcerting, as you are left to ponder what in the world you have done that has precipitated a significant concern. Fortunately, I had some pressing matters to attend to, and in a short time, I was able to let the matter completely go by the wayside. For the balance of the day, I didn't have another thought about the upcoming talk. It's funny how we can sometimes push a concern completely out of our mind, but we can only block it out for a time. My time ran out as I got home that evening and pulled into our driveway.

It is interesting to me how a person can become delusional when the prospect of having to confront an undesirable situation is placed before them. When I was twelve years old, I was given the assignment to speak in church. That notice came weeks in advance, so I had more than sufficient time to prepare. But putting off the hard stuff is something I was always able to do well, and so it was that the day arrived, with me being totally unprepared.

I was to speak that evening and, despite the need to give appropriate attention to the matter at hand, all through the day I managed to put off the preparing of my remarks. The sand in the hourglass continued to steadily drain away until only two hours remained before the starting time of the meeting.

At that point, with desperation becoming more heightened by the minute, you do begin to become delusional. You think that maybe a terrific storm would arise, possibly even a tornado, that would end up canceling the meeting ... or perhaps I could feign being sick and my mom would require that I stay home. In that situation, any possible intervention will do. I was grasping at straws.

My list of possible scenarios that would save me was soon exhausted, and I had to face reality. I had to speak for ten minutes to an audience, and I had absolutely no idea what I was going to say. I finally came across some interesting articles relating to church history and proceeded to prepare the text of my presentation.

At the service, I was the first on the program to speak. I was surprised at how, with little preparation, my talk seemed to come off without a hitch. As I returned to my seat, I enjoyed a moment of relief and a bit of satisfaction at having pulled off the impossible. But the feeling of the moment was to be fleeting.

As the remaining speakers came forward and addressed the congregation, it probably came as no surprise to anyone present that those who followed on the program focused most of their shared thoughts about their fathers. Perhaps I was the only one in the congregation who had forgotten it was Father's Day. Dad never expressed any disappointment in my choice of topic for that talk. That says a lot about my father.

That experience now came to my mind as I sat in the driveway, having some delusional thoughts about the possibility that the reason for my wife's call earlier that morning had been of no consequence and needed no attention.

Any foolish thoughts like that quickly evaporated as I came through the back door of our home and entered the kitchen. There stood my wife with a look that gave me pause. With no prelude, she simply pointed to the hallway that led to the front rooms of the first floor of our home and said, "Let's go to the living room." That wasn't good.

The living room in our home could more accurately be described as an uncomfortable sitting room. It was the room we invited guests to be seated in if we wanted their stay to be brief. It was a sizable room with formal furniture, a piano, built-in library shelves and a fireplace. In silence, my wife and I seated ourselves, with each of us in one of the two overstuffed high-backed chairs. Though it was mere seconds, it seemed like a lengthy interlude before my wife was able to gather her thoughts and speak. She began with just two words … your son.

Did any two words ever come to the human ear bringing any greater relief than those two just spoken by my wife? Well, probably, but at that particular moment, you would have been hard pressed to share any that would have topped the ones I had just heard.

I concealed the sigh of relief that so needed to be released. So, it wasn't me who was in trouble. It was my son who was the guilty party. But guilty of what? My mind raced, thinking of the possible dastardly deeds a five-year-old could possibly commit. I thought, and hoped, he was way too young for the concern to be girl-related. No, his four sisters were regularly disabusing him of any thoughts of girls being enjoyable to be around.

Maybe it was something to do with playing with fire. From my personal experiences, I knew that all boys are born pyromaniacs. Well, as I'd arrived home, I didn't see any smoke. The detached garage and house both seemed to be intact. Apparently, playing with fire wasn't the concern.

It was about that time, having mentally eliminated some of the more probable possible concerns, that my wife continued, "Your son had some of his little friends over today." Warning signs began to flash in my head.

There are times when a word is used to define a "something," as opposed to just being descriptive. I have found that it can be somewhat concerning when a wife uses the adjective "little." It can be of even more concern when the possessive "your" is found paired with that particular adjective in the same sentence. Your little friend, your little job, your little trip, or your little ball game. You probably get the picture. Usually not a good thing.

My son was in double jeopardy, and I was concerned that I might not be far behind.

She continued, "They were playing in the strip of woods that borders our property, and I had not heard anything from them in a while. So, I went out to check on them." Rule number one with young boys: If they are playing, and no one is screaming in pain, leave them alone. But my wife felt the need to check on them. Big mistake.

As she approached the woods, she heard excited chatter. She thought it sounded like the boys were having a good time. They were. In that strip of timber, in a small clearing by the kids' playhouse, is a large oak tree. It measures every bit of five feet at the base, with a height approaching sixty feet or more. As my wife entered that clearing, to her horror, she found five little boys standing around the large oak tree, having the time of their little lives, urinating in unison.

Now, you have to understand, this was our first and only son. My wife had no brothers, and her folks never were much into camping out in the wild. She was somewhat unacquainted with the habits of boys in need of relieving themselves when no restroom facilities are conveniently present. As she related what had taken place, I could see that what she had witnessed had been most disturbing to her.

My wife inquired as to what I proposed should be done relative to instruction, and possible discipline, of our son. The situation called for a sensitive and appropriate response. I sensed that from her perspective, a lengthy jail sentence or burning at the stake were possible appropriate measures. Upon being informed that the boy was up in his room, I indicated that I would immediately have a serious sit-down visit with him.

My son's room was located at the top of the second-floor stairs. As I knocked and entered his room, I found him playing on the floor with some of his toys. I said to him, "Son, I understand you had some of your friends over to play today." In his most innocent voice, he replied, "Yeah, Dad, we had fun." I continued, "Mom said you were all playing out in the woods around the playhouse."

Continuing to play with his toys, completely ignorant of the significant danger he was in, he said, "Yeah, we had a great time playing out by the playhouse, Dad." After a thoughtful pause, I said, "Son, can you do me a favor? Can you make sure when you boys need to pee on the big oak tree, that there are no girls around ... especially your mom?" He slowly turned his attention to me and, with a quizzical look on his face, nodded slowly in the affirmative.

As I stood and was about to leave the room, I turned and with one last thoughtful pause said, "Son, when you are a little older, we'll have another conversation ... about girls and that big oak tree."

That was another kind of worry, which I knew could be put off for another day ... and most likely would probably involve another phone call.

Charlie

IT WAS ON THE first day on the job that I was introduced to Charlie. I didn't actually meet Charlie that day. The introduction came by way of a conversation with Henry, my new boss.

I had accepted the general manager position at a country club. In that role, I reported directly to Henry, who was the president of the club's board of directors. I was in my office working at my desk that Saturday morning when Henry stopped by for some conversation. He had just finished his Saturday morning round of golf, and there was a problem that he felt required action on our part.

There had been a dispute between two club members on the first tee earlier that morning that nearly erupted into more than just a polite argument. Hearing Charlie's name, as one of the members involved in that dispute, would be that first introduction.

Henry thought a letter from the club manager might be appropriate. I suggested that since both individuals involved were longtime members, an approach to each of them by someone who knew them well might be a more effective way of addressing the concern. Henry followed through with that suggestion, and I was later left with the impression that the matter had been resolved. It would be the first of many interactions relating to Charlie that would occur over the next few years.

Upon coming aboard, I was told that, in general, the previous manager had been very effective, and operations were running smoothly. However, Henry shared with me that there was one area of concern that would probably need attention, that being the need to improve the performance of the club's golf professional. The way in which that concern was shared left me with the impression that replacement of the pro might be the more preferred approach to resolving the issue.

Sure enough, eighteen months later, I found myself in a board meeting where discussing the golf professional's contract was the main topic on the agenda. The prior year, in an effort to reposition the club's financial relationship with the golf professional, an employment contract had been put into place. The thrust of that change was to realign the relationship with the pro into a clearer contractual agreement. The hope was for an improved level of service for the membership in that area of the operation.

In my report, I shared that I felt some progress had been made in the club's relationship with the pro. As the board conversation evolved, I quickly realized that I was pretty much standing alone in that assessment.

In turn, each of the seven board members present expressed significant concerns about retaining our golf professional. The final nail in the coffin was driven by a story related by one of our younger, newer board members. Marshall, a successful businessman, had come into the community, married and was raising a family who were active at the club. He was a good tennis player, who was enjoying learning the game of golf. Eventually, he would become a good single-digit handicap player. Taking golf lessons with our pro was moving him along in that direction.

However, he related that after a recent lesson, our golf professional had noted that he had just one suggestion for his new protégé. Marshall shared that he thought the pro's suggestions might include recommending the need to alter his stance or grip on the club, or possibly modify something in the motion of his swing. But the pro's suggestion was simply that he thought that Marshall should play more tennis.

The primary focus of a golf professional is to promote the playing of the game, to have club members enjoy and play more golf. The truth of the matter is that the pro was no doubt making the comment in jest. But Marshall hadn't taken his comment that way, and the experience fit neatly into the evolving consensus that it was time for the club to make a change. The following week, I was sitting in my office with the club president as we shared the news with our golf professional that his contract was not going to be renewed.

The fact was, there would have been a number of members who welcomed that change. It's impossible to please everyone. However, it was also true that there were those who thought the pro was doing a satisfactory job. Charlie would have been one who retained an appreciation of, and support for, the pro. So, relative to the possibility of Charlie and me being able to progress toward developing a positive relationship, the release of the golf professional was somewhat problematic.

There were rumors of a possible petition that might be circulated to support retention of the pro. Though nothing came of that, I could sense in my interactions with Charlie that he wasn't sure the right decision had been made. Charlie had a way of having conversations happen mostly when—and in the way—he wanted them. Our conversations in the coming months were mostly limited to concerns relating to food quality at the club when Charlie came out for lunch. Most times on greeting Charlie, in return I would receive a combination of a muffled grunt and a subtle version of a scowl. Interactions with Charlie weren't to be one of my favorite things for the moment.

It was about that time that a new board member was elected to serve on the club's board of directors. Bob, a partner in a number of Wendy's fast-food restaurants, was a natural choice to serve as chair of our Food & Beverage Committee. I soon began working with Bob to sort out possible approaches to address food service concerns at the club. As our conversations would turn to dining experiences at the club, I fairly quickly became aware that Bob and Charlie had lunch together on a regular basis. In fact, their routines included lunch at the club nearly every day. On Mondays, when the club would be closed, they would often have lunch together at one of Bob's restaurant locations. I gradually developed an impression that Charlie had a tight circle of people with whom he shared closed interactions. Working with Bob became a part of the process of coming to better understand Charlie.

In conversations with Bob, I admitted that I had a hard time figuring Charlie out. Bob would always simply say that Charlie was alright. Though I didn't realize it at the time, the journey of understanding Charlie had begun. Another year passed, and another new board member came along who would continue to move that process forward in a positive way.

Tony was a well-thought-of community leader and successful businessman. He had been asked to chair the Green Committee, the committee that had oversight responsibility for maintenance of the golf course. As Tony was going about reorganizing his committee, he stopped me in the clubhouse one day and asked if I would have any objections to Charlie becoming a member of his committee. I have to admit that my first thought was that I wasn't sure I was excited about the prospect of sitting in a meeting with Charlie every month. But I had come to understand that Charlie had a love for both the game and his club's golf course. I knew that the Green Committee would be a good place for him to serve.

I was a little more than surprised that, from the very first committee meeting, I began to see another side of Charlie. I would have thought that he might be one who would have an agenda and constantly be promoting what he would like to see done. However, I found Charlie to be measured in his comments, concise in his analysis and consistent in looking not just after his own particular interests but the best interests of the club.

Over time, I gradually began to see Charlie as not just an effective contributor at committee level but someone to be considered for service on the board of directors. It was just a couple of years later that Charlie was asked to serve in that capacity. He eventually filled two terms as club president, the first member of his club to be extended that particular honor.

Over time, as I worked with Charlie, I came to appreciate several qualities that he possessed. He had good business instincts and a confidence level that allowed him to be decisive in taking action. He was good at reading people. I am not sure that I ever knew anyone who was better at that than Charlie. Last, he was the kind of giver that I respected. There are those who give, and everyone around them knows who the giver is and how much has been given. Charlie was a giver, but when he gave, he didn't necessarily require any recognition. In fact, in my experience, I observed that he usually shunned public notice, or credit, as he served his club and community.

Along the way, the understanding that we both had the best interests of the club at heart allowed what had been an uneasy alliance to eventually develop into a relationship of mutual trust and respect.

It was a few years later, as I was preparing to leave my employment at the club, that Charlie stopped by my office for some conversation. We shared some stories and rehashed some of the moments. As Charlie was about to go, I let him know how much I had appreciated the opportunity to work with him. More importantly, I let him know how much I appreciated his allowing me to have some time to get to know him. Being a private person, I am not sure he allowed too many people to do that, to see the real Charlie. I considered myself fortunate to have had that experience.

It was a number of years later that I came back into town to attend my mother's funeral service. I called Charlie's office to see if I could catch up with him while I was in town. His assistant told me he had seen the notice of Mom's passing and was planning on being at the visitation that evening. Sure enough, at the appointed time, Charlie arrived. He and one of my best friends from my youth stood by my side the whole evening.

Following the visitation, Charlie and I were discussing old times and some of what had taken place in the intervening years since we had worked together. I thought to ask him a question I had often wondered about. Since I'd left the club a number of years earlier, Charlie had been one of the references I listed on an attachment that accompanied my professional resume. I would always have six individuals on that list, and they would change from time to time as my career working relationships moved along. But Charlie was the one constant. He had always been one of the six.

So, at a pause in the conversation, I asked my question, "Charlie, being one of my references, you probably received several phone calls over the years. In those conversations, what would you share about your time working with me?"

Without hesitating, Charlie responded and said, "Bo, I always just tell them that you saved our club." He went on to say that the improvements made to the club during our time working together on the board had well positioned the club for the future. The club was better prepared to weather the storm when changes in the marketplace came.

Though I appreciated Charlie's response to the question, I felt it was more a generous, heartfelt expression than an accurate assessment. I had come to that club early in my career, full of confidence and thinking that I knew a few things. The challenge when you are young is not to let your ego get ahead of your knowledge and experience. It was during that time of working with Charlie that my experience began to catch up with my ego, as I began to understand just how little I really knew and how much more there was to learn.

I did, however, leave that club knowing a couple of things for sure. I knew I had learned more about the journey of finding the best in other people and how that can allow for productive relationships to develop. More importantly, I had learned that those experiences may come in ways that you might least expect, and sometimes you end up finding not just another mentor but also a friend.

Along the way, Charlie had done that for me. Looking back, I could only hope I had been able to do some of that for him.

That's what friends do.

Change Driver

IT'S BEEN SAID THAT there are two things in life that are certain … death and taxes. There is at least one other of life's certainties that should be added to the list: the certainty of change.

Change seems to come about in two ways. There is change that comes completely independent of anything we may do, and then there is the change that is generated by action on our part. We have little control of the former, with much more freedom of choice and agency relative to the latter.

The Serenity Prayer, written by American theologian Reinhold Niebuhr, helps bring into focus how we might have positive thought and action relative to change. "God, grant me the serenity to accept the things I cannot change, courage to change the things I can, and wisdom to know the difference." Ah, that wisdom thing.

If you were to speak to anyone who knew much about my management experience in the private club industry, the first thing they might share is that I was a financial guy. I was fortunate to be able to bring positive financial change to each of the clubs I managed. It's a bit ironic, given that failing performance back in my eighth grade math class. To say the least, Mr. Simmons would be more than a bit surprised. Along the way I did learn the importance of applying myself in my studies. More importantly, there was something that allowed me to see numbers in a different way. With the placement of a dollar sign by a number, suddenly it became a different thing. Something very different.

The English band Depeche Mode has a song that I particularly like. "Everything Counts" is a song about the handling of money with the lyrical refrain, "Everything counts in large amounts." I guess I owe some of my success in the business world to learning how to make everything count. But the most significant positive change I experienced was really more about the change that comes about in people … not money.

A few years back, I had come into a club that had just gone through a significant amount of turmoil. The board had felt that they needed to terminate the previous manager. Due to the sensitive nature of the separation, from a legal standpoint, they had not been able to share much about the reason supporting their decision. The result was a lingering question among the membership relative to confidence in the recent board decision.

For the moment, my primary objective was the calming of the waters and the sorting out of operational changes that needed to be implemented. As I became acclimated to the club staff and membership, I fairly quickly came to trust and depend on Delores, the club's food and beverage director. She had been at the club for many years and knew where many of the skeletons were hidden in the closets. More importantly, she knew which ones not to bother.

Late one evening, at the end of a long busy day, I stopped by Delores's office to chat. I was just checking in to see how things were going and was looking for not just a recap of the day but also some unwinding conversation that would provide a little stress relief. What transpired wasn't to be one of those kinds of sessions.

As our conversation progressed that evening, I could sense that Delores was hesitant about sharing something with me. As I patiently allowed the conversation to run its course, Delores finally brought up the concern that was on her mind. She said, "You know, Bo, Tom doesn't really like you."

Tom, a club member, was one of the prominent business leaders in the community. He had built a successful company and accumulated some wealth. Like you find in many small-town environments, people notice and pay some attention to those who make things happen. Tom was one of those people who made things happen … he was one of the big fish in the small pond of that community.

I had met Tom, but our occasional interaction had been limited to the casual "Hello, how are you doing?" kind of greetings. In observing his activity at the club, it seemed that he had a small clique that made up his close-knit social circle. I also came to understand that he had a temper that could flare up hot and fast. It had not happened yet in my short time at the club, but on frequent occasions in the past, Tom would make his way into the club kitchen if his meal was less than to his satisfaction or if it was taking longer to prepare than he thought it should. The staff were in constant fear of the next episode that could come at any time.

My read was that his circle of friends on occasion had to look past his behavior and that possibly the reason they were willing to do that had something to do with how much influence Tom had in the community ... and perhaps how much money he had in his bank account.

I inquired of Delores as to why she thought Tom might have an unfavorable opinion of me. She shared that she had the impression that Tom didn't like some of the changes I was implementing. I thanked her for bringing the concern to my attention and, for the moment, set aside any further thoughts about it. At that point in my career, I had learned enough to know that if you spent too much time thinking about what you had to do to have everyone like you, you could end up in the crazy house.

It was, however, a worry that began occupying my thoughts. Some have credited Abraham Lincoln with the oft quoted saying, "You can please some of the people all of the time, and all of the people some of the time ... but you can't please all of the people all of the time." I am not really sure that

Honest Abe was the original author who had come up with that thought. It was probably some frustrated Neanderthal when groups of more than two began to gather and try to come to some important decision, like whether the mammoth steak should be served medium rare or well done. In any event, as I thought more about it, I wasn't sure that Tom was going to be one who I was going to be able to please even some of the time.

I hadn't had time to give Delores's revelation much further thought when, just a week later, I wandered into the club pub late one evening to find Tom and several of his friends discussing the events of the day. It crossed my mind that maybe I was one of the "events of the day" who could have been a subject of the conversation before I entered the room. As I would occasionally do, I pulled up a seat at the bar and ordered my usual, a Diet Coke on the rocks. I had no particular thought, plan or intention at that moment. I was just looking to enjoy a soft drink and some polite conversation.

However, things didn't exactly play out that way, as shortly after I sat down, one by one, everyone found a reason to call it a day and head home. Patsy, our bartender, made the last call and, before I knew it, Tom and I were the only two remaining as we finished off our drinks. The thought came to me—with just the two of us left in the room, would Tom take this opportunity to speak his mind and let me know just what he thought about me and the job I was doing?

I didn't have to wonder about that for too long, for only a couple of minutes had passed when Tom said, "You know, Bo, there are some folks around the club who aren't sure they like some of the changes you are making." *Well*, I thought, *what a relief.* Maybe it wasn't Tom who was upset with me but some other members. But just as quickly as it had come, I dismissed that foolish thought.

Pausing for just a moment, as I pondered how I might proceed, I could see some honest conversation coming. I was hoping that it wouldn't get too unpleasant. But that is something you can't always control, and sometimes folks just have to say what they think has to be said.

I shared with Tom that I could understand—and appreciate—that some folks might be uncomfortable with some things. After all, most of us really don't like change, especially when we aren't the ones making the changes. However, I went on to say that I hadn't come into town to make friends; I was there to do a job and to move the club along in the best possible way.

Continuing with that line of thought, I said, "Tom, I hope that I can develop some good relationships here, but there are some changes that need to be made, and that may cost me the opportunity of making some new friends. In fact, when I am finished here, I may leave this town having made no new friends." Then I did what they always say a good trial lawyer does—not that I have any particular fondness for trial lawyers. I asked Tom a question I thought I knew the answer to. In a calm, measured way, looking Tom square in the eye, I asked him, "Tom, how many friends do you have?" I have to admit, I had some definite thought about what the answer to that question should be.

I had crossed the Rubicon but, unlike Caesar, I didn't have a legion behind me. It was just Tom and me sitting down the bar from each other. It seemed like an eternity, but only seconds passed before Tom responded to my question with a completely unexpected answer. He simply said, "I am not sure I have any friends, Bo."

I really hadn't planned on asking that question, and I surely didn't expect to get that answer. At that moment, I had Tom right where I would have liked to have had him. With an honest response of how he truly felt, he had left himself wide open and placed himself right into my hands. His admission that perhaps he had no true friends placed a number of possible options at my disposal for my follow-up.

I could have told Tom the worst possible reasons that what he said might be true. The sharing of my least sensitive thoughts could have gone something like, "Well, no wonder you don't have any friends, Tom, you are such a pathetic, selfish, narcissistic, ill-tempered brute," or any other heartless comments that my mind might conjure up.

I was amazed at the next words that, with almost no hesitation, came out my mouth. In response to Tom's honest, humble self-appraisal that he may not have a true friend in the world, I simply said, "Well, Tom, maybe both of us are in the same boat." There was some truth to that admission. When you are driving change, even when you are doing the right thing, not everyone is going to be comfortable with the ride.

I was only at that club a few months more after that conversation between Tom and me. I like to think that the conversation we had was a positive moment of change for both of us. Maybe Tom understood me a little better. I know the honest conversation we shared allowed me to see and appreciate Tom in a different way. It is something I have never forgotten.

Perhaps Depeche Mode got it right. Everything does count in large amounts, especially the learning moments about others … and yourself. Sometimes driving the change that needs to happen doesn't come easy … and sometimes on that ride, the good change is the one that can come in you.

Part Three
Reconciliation

I THINK THERE IS no denying that we live in a crazy, mixed-up world. We all play our part in making it that way. It has been said that in this world the "normal" people are just the crazy people you don't know well enough. We should all take comfort in knowing that there really is no such thing as normal. We are all alike in that respect, each of us offering our individual unique self to the world.

Another thing that we have in common is that we all face our own share of personal challenges.

Sometimes the weight that rests upon our shoulders can seem unbearable. We may think that we are the only ones who are having to deal with what we have on our plate. But most people are good at hiding their problems, doubts and fears. I think Henry David Thoreau had it right when he wrote, "The mass of men lead lives of quiet desperation."

Sometimes we may look at another and think that it might be nice to trade our life for theirs. But the reality is that, in most cases, we would simply be trading one set of challenges for another.

There is at least one more thing we all have in common: the never-ending search for that thing we call happiness. It's been said that happiness, or at least peace, is the sense that nothing is missing in the moment. I like that thought.

Reconciling the meaning of the moments that come along in life can play a part in leading us to that place of contentment, understanding and peace. That happens when we uncover the connection between the experience of the moment and the lesson we may learn from it.

Life is a journey, not an event. Reconciliation of the purpose in it all is something to be found along the way.

Last Drive North

When I was a young boy, I hated long trips. Our visits to see family back home in Kentucky involved a five-hour journey in the back seat of the family car. The ride there was tolerable, because of the excitement of seeing my grandparents, aunts, uncles and cousins. The return trip was filled with the sadness of separation. That drive home seemed to take forever.

On long drives, Dad could assume the attributes of a camel. He seemed to have unusual endurance, as he could go for hours without food or water. When he was focused on the destination, nothing could pull him off the road. Somewhere along the line, in later years, things changed for me, and I found a way to develop some ability to endure the long drive, just like Dad.

And so, it was on a cold winter day that I found myself beginning a seven-hour journey. I was traveling from my home in Eastern Kentucky for my first visit to Grand Rapids, Michigan. This wasn't a trip for pleasure. It was all business. I would be interviewing for a possible job the next morning.

I could have booked a flight for the trip. But I wanted some time for pondering. I was making this drive alone, with some quiet time to consider the coming interview. Seven hours on the road was giving me that quiet time.

I didn't have to make this possible job change. I was in a good spot at my current club, but I had reached all that I should be asking for in the way of my compensation package. I knew if I was going to make one more good move in my career, the time was right. I was fifty-five years old, and the clock was ticking. I had one more move, but it had to be the right one.

I was about a half hour into the drive when I began to focus my thoughts on the upcoming meeting with the search committee. As I drove along, my mind began going through the paces of how the interview would flow. I had reviewed the documents that the search firm had sent along earlier that week. Included in the packet was information on club history, governance structure, membership and the club's current financial position. Going over that information in my mind, I settled into my thoughts on how I was seeing the opportunity and making sure I felt that the fit was right for me. I then turned to the other side of the equation. How would the search committee see me as being the right fit for the club? After all, the successful hire must include a matchup that works for both the company and the candidate.

As I drove the next few miles down the road, I quickly went down the checklist of what I thought the qualifications for the position were and how I might see myself stacking up. I then came to the one final question that I knew would come in the interview.

All the candidates would come with experience, knowledge and skills that they had developed in their prior positions of responsibility. They would not have made it through the hoops the recruiting firm put them through unless their qualifications were solid. The final question that had to be answered in the interview would be, "Why me?"

Why would I be the one who was different enough to end up being the committee's final choice?

As I went down that checklist, comparing myself to the other candidates, I asked myself that question. One by one, I had to reject the obvious possible specific qualifications that would separate me from the others. We all had to be competent in the primary proficiencies, or we wouldn't be there. I thought to myself, *Will this simply come down to how I handle the interview, the likability factor or how I come across as Mr. Personality?*

It was then that another thought came that had never been present in my mind in prior interviews or conversations. There was one quality that I wasn't sure everyone else in the interview process would possess … at least not in the way it affected me. It was the knowledge and confidence I had that when I was paying attention to my spiritual side, it made me a different person … a stronger person … actually, to the point that I felt unbeatable.

As that thought came to mind, I immediately pushed it aside. An expression of that kind could have me coming across as either someone with an out-of-control ego … or a religious fanatic. I didn't feel I was either of those, but in a meeting with complete strangers, I might find myself leaving a very negative first impression. Sharing that thought could very well push me off the table as a viable candidate for consideration. As I drove down the road, my search for the possible difference-maker continued.

But try as I may, every effort to come up with another differentiating quality failed. Over the course of the next couple of hours, I kept coming back to the same conclusion as to what could possibly separate me from the others. I finally came to understand that this trip may not be about me having a job-changing opportunity.

I was being told exactly what I should say in that interview, and it had nothing to do with any counsel offered to me by a recruiting firm. Knowing that became the only thing that really mattered. The thought occurred to me that perhaps I was on a three-day adventure, driving over a thousand miles, so that these folks would hear that one sentence. Who knows, maybe there would be just one person present who needed to hear what I now knew I had to say.

And true to form, in the interview the following day, the usual round of questions came from the search committee. I suppose my responses probably closely resembled those given by the other candidates. Then, close to the end of the interview, what I knew would come … came. One of the committee members asked the question, "Why you, Bo?"

My reply was the easiest interview response I have ever had to give, not that it brought any comfort to me. I tried to have some humility as I responded to the question and simply said, "I am sure all of the candidates in this process are very qualified. The one way I may be different is that I know that I am a stronger person when I am paying attention to my spiritual side." I continued, "In fact, I know that when I am doing that, I am unbeatable."

There was no visible reaction from the nine committee members sitting around the table … nothing, just silence. Following that pronouncement, I don't even remember the last question or two that came from the committee chairperson. Then, as the floor was given to individual committee members to have one last question, a lady sitting directly across the table from me began her comments by saying, "Now Bo, we realize you are a religious person." I interrupted her by saying, "I didn't mean to imply that I am a religious person, or necessarily a good person. I have just come to understand that when I am paying attention to my spiritual side, I experience an empowering change. I feel I become more aware of the person I truly have the potential to be."

On the long drive home, I had plenty of time to reflect on the interview. I took comfort in knowing that I had said what I was supposed to say. I had no confidence that I was going to be offered the job, but there was a strange peace in it all. The job opportunity may have been lost, but I felt that there must have been a greater purpose that was being served. I was content in doing what I felt I had been asked to do.

I was more than a bit surprised when I received an early call the next day from Kurt, my contact with the recruiting firm.

To be honest, I really didn't expect it. It's always a positive sign when you receive some immediate follow-up to an interview. Rejections usually come days later, after the preferred candidate has come to a contractual agreement with the company and the search is formally closed. So the early morning call was a good omen.

However, despite my initial optimism, the conversation quickly took an unpleasant turn as Kurt shared that he had some good news and some bad news. With those words, my heart sank. This was not going to be the call I was hoping for.

Well, I always like to get the bad stuff out of the way first, so I asked, "What's the bad news, Kurt?" At that point, I just wanted to wrap up the call and avoid the words of solace and encouragement that a recruiter gives you when you don't make the cut. His answer to my inquiry came without any hesitation on his part, "Well, you ended up being the number two choice." That was the answer I'd anticipated, but before I could give that any thought, he continued by saying, "The good news is that they want to have the top two candidates come back for a second interview."

My immediate reaction was to let Kurt know that I wasn't too excited about making another fourteen-hour round trip just to repeat my second-place performance. Of course, he went right into all the positives, "Bo, they really liked you. You interviewed well. You are a good fit for this club."

As he continued in this vein, the reminder quickly came to my mind that this interview was probably not about me being offered the job. It was about the delivering of a message.

So, though I really had no thought about experiencing a different result, I ended up with no reluctance in accepting the opportunity to return for that second interview. As I drove up to meet with the committee for a second time, I found myself very comfortable knowing that my assignment was really pretty simple. I would answer the questions the committee had for me, but I knew what the real message was that needed to be delivered.

Sure enough, the second interview was very similar to the first. There were some new faces around the table, but the format was much like the initial interview session. Near the end of the interview, the question came again: "Bo, why are you the one?" In a comfortable and confident tone, I once again shared what I had been told to share.

The interview concluded shortly after, and with that, I thought I had done what I had been sent there to do. Though my personal job search was to continue, at that moment I never felt better about an anticipated prospect of being rejected.

There was no way I was expecting a call from Kurt the next day that would inform me that I was the committee's choice for the hire.

But that call came.

A couple of months later, I was conversing with Gail, the search committee chairperson. As she was a person of faith, I felt prompted to have some conversation with her about the experience of the interview process.

After I had finished relating my side of the story, she shared hers. She told me that in the first round, I had interviewed well, but the other candidate had come across a little stronger. However, she related that in the second round, it was quite different. In her words, I had just blown the committee away in the interview, and they felt completely comfortable with offering the position to me.

I had accepted the offer and opportunity. Little did I know as I embarked on that journey that there were many trials ahead. I knew much about the challenges the club was facing at the moment. What I didn't count on was the impending complete collapse of the economy, along with myriad other storms related to that recession that were on the horizon.

I could write a chapter about every club that I have had the opportunity to serve. This club experience would require a book. I have often paused to reflect that if the extent of the challenges had been revealed to me in the interview process, I would have had to admit that I had no knowledge, or experience, that would have prepared me for what lay ahead.

Making the things happen that needed to happen were, in part, due to the efforts of some great members and staff leaders. However, I have never failed to acknowledge that none of us individually, or collectively, could have done all that was needed to be done relying only on ourselves. The only explanation was Providence. Therein is where the credit is due.

I no longer mind long drives. I have also learned that I don't always have to finish first. Relative to the unusual circumstances involved on that long drive that day, I thought the message I was carrying was for someone on a search committee. That may have been the case. That was a possibility. But, in the end, sometimes the carrier of the message is the one that ends up being the one that the message is most intended for.

It took a couple of long drives north to help me find my way to understanding that I don't always need to be the one behind the wheel. In this case, staying on the right track had nothing to do with me being the driver, but about understanding more about the one who is always in control.

What's Love Got to Do with It?

THERE ARE TIMES, MOMENTS, when I think that perhaps as I was growing up, my dad ruined me.

I saw Dad as a hard-working, responsible father who was always concerned about making sure our family was provided for. It seemed he could do and fix anything, from washing machines to well pumps. His work ethic was ever-present, almost intimidating, as it seemed he was always working at getting something done that needed to be done.

I am not sure that I ever had a feeling that Dad loved his job. But there seemed to be something about keeping busy doing things that gave him some satisfaction. On more than one occasion, I remember him sharing with me that work isn't work if you are enjoying what you are doing. I often wondered if I could ever measure up to the example he was setting for us … learn to enjoy work and be as productive as he was.

One of the takeaways from the experience was the feeling that I had to work to earn my play … that I had to get my work done before I could take time off. Later in life, as I tried to make time for my family, I was to discover that balancing work and play didn't happen by accident and required some thought and planning. I know there were too many times that I failed in that … and once the moments pass, they are gone forever. Relative to my children, I learned the hard way that sometimes the lesson you think you are teaching ends up not being the lesson they end up learning.

When they are young, you are giving them constant direction, from helping them with the clothes they wear and the meals they eat, to deciding for them the places they will go and the things they should be involved in doing. In some respects, those are the easier days of parenting … you do the providing, you set the rules and you do the teaching. Along the way, you try to have them understand the things that you think are important.

At some point, they become more independent in their thinking, wanting to make their own decisions and become their own person. You have suddenly become less knowledgeable, and they are less interested in the things you have to share. That's when parenting gets a bit more complicated, and you have to watch for the teaching moments. Most of the time, those opportune moments are dictated by them, not you. And on occasion, you walk away from the conversation … with them having been the teacher, not you.

I was at home having lunch with our two youngest daughters one day when the opportunity came along to have one of those kinds of conversations. At the time, they were college age and had both arrived at that time in their life where some definite opinions had been—and were continuing to be—formed. It was partway through that conversation when I saw an opening to ask a question that had been on my mind for some time.

Over the years, my career path required much of my time and energy. As a manager, responsible for running an operation, there were times when there were long and unusual hours required. In my mind, I always felt that I had become somewhat like my dad in that I didn't necessarily love my job but was just being responsible in providing for my family.

I knew that my family was not sure that was always the case, that the time I invested in my work responsibilities was a confirmation that there might not be anything more important to me than my job. And so, when the opening in the conversation presented itself that day, I asked my daughters a question, "Girls, do you think your dad loves his job?"

My next-to-youngest daughter was the "truth-teller" in our family. Though she had always been somewhat shy and reserved, it was her nature to be honest and not restrained in expressing her opinion, especially if she thought there was something of importance that needed to be said. She was immediate in her response to my question, announcing without any hesitation, "Oh yeah, Dad, you love your job!"

Her response to my question came as no surprise, and I could sense that her sister concurred with the assessment. To me there was some irony in the impression that my daughters held. I never had the thought that I loved my job. It was something that I could do well enough, but for me it was simply the vehicle that enabled me to provide for my family.

So, I was quick to ask a follow-up question, "What is it that makes you think I really love my job?" Again, the response from my truth-teller was immediate: "Dad, you just love telling people what to do." Any parent can understand where that impression could have originated. Giving our children direction on a regular basis comes with the territory.

I immediately, without any hesitation, followed up with an observation of my own. I shared the thought, which I had always known, that I would rather be the one doing the telling than the one being told. I felt confident that line of thought was something they could relate to.

At that moment, I marked in my mind the brief interchange, a conversation that I thought brought about a moment of truth. No, I told myself, I didn't really love my job. It was just the way that I was able to provide for my family. To me, my club management career had been what my dad would have called work. It was a job that needed to be done, and following my father's example, I was just doing what needed to be done. It was a simple, satisfying answer to what I thought was a question that shouldn't have needed to be asked.

It would have been nice if the issue had been put to bed that day. But that wasn't the case. I found that, from time to time, the memory of that conversation would return. As I revisited the exchange between my daughters and myself, I would find some satisfaction in the recounting. Yet there remained a haunting feeling that the conversation was left unfinished, with the question yet unanswered. Several years would pass before the process would begin for another epiphanous moment to bring some unexpected clarity for me.

It happened as I was preparing an outline for an upcoming presentation; I was once again reminded of that past conversation with my daughters. The subject at hand had to do with the connection between passion and performance. As I was once more giving the interaction of that day some thoughtful consideration, my mind returned to that lingering question, *Do I really love my job?* Allowing my thoughts to dive just a bit deeper for an answer, another troubling question rose to the surface. If I didn't love my job, how was I able to manage that career path successfully for more than thirty years?

It was a question that deserved an answer, and with some additional thought, I came to some surprising conclusions. No, I didn't really love my job. But I began to understand that there were aspects of my work that I really did love. That revelation was a bit unsettling. Maybe my thoughts about it had been wrong all along.

At that point, I realized I needed to take some time to identify and better understand what it was about my work that allowed passion to not just make periodic appearances but be a part of my regular routine. I thought I could get there in the time it would take to finish up my presentation prep. The search that I thought would take hours ended up taking more than a year.

In the final analysis, I discovered eight things in my work that were key motivators that could drive me. I came to think of them as my "Crazy Eights." They are the things that could have been found in all the varied aspects of my life and in any career path that I would have chosen. They are what allowed me to get through the difficult moments, the challenging situations … the occasional times when I would just want to walk away and find another job.

They are the eight things I discovered that I loved about my work. I love …

1. Doing something that not everyone can do well.
2. The challenge of finding the way to the win.
3. Finding the good in a person, where the good is less apparent.
4. Being a part of something that is greater than myself.
5. The mentoring experience that comes through association with others.
6. The illusion of being in control.
7. Organizing and the creating of order.
8. The journey of better understanding self and the process of becoming better.

Well, I have to admit that my dad didn't really ruin me, and he was right about a job not being work if it is something you enjoy doing. I must admit my girls were right, too. I had been wrong all those years. Love did have something to do with it. But I didn't really love my job … just those "crazy eight" pieces of it where purpose was found, and passion uncovered.

Another unexpected part of the discovery process was coming to understand how much each of those eight were drivers that could, and should, have also been a significant part of my family relationships. In retrospect, I am left to ask myself how much that didn't happen. Sorting out those pieces is something I regret not having figured out sooner.

Coming to understand where one's passions lie—not just the things that you enjoy or can do well, but those things that really drive you—is a lesson worth learning. All sorts of good things can come from that kind of knowledge.

That's when love will have everything to do with it.

Did God Make Santa?

THE FULL MAILBOX OF letters for Santa in the lobby entrance of the club was just another reminder that the Christmas season was upon us. Every year we would collect and forward hundreds of letters from all the boys and girls (and a few bad old men) to Santa. I had the enjoyable and enviable job of getting to read each and every one of those letters. It was one of my perks as a club manager.

The various comments and expressions you may find in letters to Santa are sometimes inciteful, often humorous and occasionally revealing. Children are taught from the time that they can talk that Santa comes once a year to little children who are good. What child really wants to fess up to not having been particularly good, and how many ways can a child really substantiate their good behavior over the past twelve months without resorting to some level of exaggeration, or outright deceit?

And at what age does a child realize that speaking an untruth may have consequences? At best, it does not appear that it happens much before the age of ten. Did one little girl really believe that not killing her brother might qualify her for some leniency from Old St. Nick?

Then, too, there are telltale signs when Mom or Dad is acting as proxy in writing the letter to Santa. The first clue is that you can actually read the letter. The correct spelling of words comes in a close second. In my experience, too many kids have trouble with their spelling, even after four years of college. Actually, relative to spelling skills, there too often seems little difference between the eight-year-old and the fifteen-year-old … just longer misspelled words.

Another way I can ferret out the proxy letter is the wish list. What child wants socks or books? That request has to be from either a mom of a preschooler or a prison inmate who has been incarcerated for a year or longer. Of course, Santa probably receives an occasional letter from a child who should be locked up.

And you know a letter could not have come from a child if they write, "I would like to be surprised." Every child has a list, and a surprise is the last thing they want. This may be quickly confirmed if a parent ever strays off the request list and has "surprise" gifts placed under the tree.

Sometimes a child resorts to expressions of desperation … as in the example of a seven-year-old's letter to Santa where the young boy declares, "My mom said I was good all the time." Moms always come through in the clutch. I think Santa knows this, so it may not be the most convincing line.

Among all of the letters I would receive each year, I would always find some that would cause me to pause and reflect. One little girl wrote, "I love Santa … he is amazing!" Amazing is an appropriate adjective for someone who spends every waking hour in a giving effort.

As little children, we first come to think of Santa as someone who brings presents for us. We experience the thrill and joy of finding presents from him under the tree on Christmas morning. Understanding the thrill that comes from receiving helps us to eventually understand the thrill that comes from the giving. And that is what makes Santa special. He helps teach us not just the joy of receiving but also the wonderful feelings that come with the giving.

Yes, Santa truly is amazing.

Perhaps the letter I remember best was submitted by a young author who simply expressed her appreciation, and wrote, "I love your presents … I love how God made Santa."

Well, the real spirit of Christmas is truly magical. It is all about the giving of gifts of love. Did God really make Santa? I really don't know how to answer that question. But I do believe that God does love the giving of gifts. He showed that love by giving us the greatest gift of all … the gift of his Son.

Give Him Another Chance

As you reflect on your life, you probably have one of two thoughts. You may feel that you have lived a life with no regret, with no thought that you want a rewind or replay. On the other hand, you may be one who has had those kinds of moments where you would like a do-over. It might have been a moment of an unkind word, or action, a decision at a fork in the road or the choice without appropriate consideration of the possible consequences. When I think about the mistakes that come in life and the finality that often comes, I am reminded of a story I heard many years ago.

Johnny was never a great student. But he was a good athlete ... a very good athlete. As he was finishing up his high school years, he had racked up plenty of awards. Numerous local newspaper articles told stories of his competitive exploits. College recruiters were continually calling and knocking on his door. The trophies on his bedroom wall were a silent testament to his most valuable player, all-conference and all-regional achievements. He wrapped up his senior year with all-state recognition in three sports. The future seemed bright.

Johnny wasn't one of those jocks who took in the accolades and eventually began believing all the hype. He was the kind of player who always gave his teammates their fair share of the credit for the win. He was an example of the ideal team player … the one who not only performs at a high level but makes everyone on his team perform just a little bit better in the process.

However, perhaps the best thing one could say about Johnny was he was just a likable kid. He had a winning personality and made friends easily. He had a genuine like for people that made it easy for others to like him. So, it wasn't the individual stats or the score at the end of the contest that made Johnny a winner. It was how he treated other people. Everyone liked Johnny.

But Johnny had a problem—a real problem. Throughout his school years, he had always made satisfactory grades. He did well in English and history and was just good enough to get by in science. But mathematics was a different story. Johnny just couldn't keep any amount of focus on any math class he ever had. He just wasn't interested enough to put in the needed study time. As a result, as graduation time approached, Johnny was failing his senior math course, and without a passing grade would not be able to graduate.

And so it was that just a few weeks before graduation day, Johnny found himself sitting in the principal's office with his mom and dad. In the awkward conversation that followed, Johnny and his parents' worst fears were confirmed. Johnny wasn't going to graduate. But Mr. Howard had a thought about how to not have this become an embarrassment for Johnny and his family. He suggested that Johnny could walk with his class at the graduation exercise, but unlike his classmates, instead of a graduation certificate enclosed in the small binder, Johnny's would have just a blank piece of paper.

Johnny and his parents were appreciative of Mr. Howard's kind gesture. Though disappointed in the situation they found themselves in, they agreed that the suggested course of action was the best way to avoid any undue attention or possible embarrassment for Johnny. Theirs was a small mountain community and people liked to talk. This was something that folks could talk about for a long time.

Johnny could always retake his math course over the summer and, if all went well, possibly pursue his college opportunity in the fall.

Well, like any small town in America, there are few private matters that remain secrets. And as parents and students gathered in the school gymnasium on graduation day, the site of so many of Johnny's extraordinary athletic moments, everyone present knew Johnny was not going to receive his diploma on this day.

As, one by one, in alphabetical order, each of Johnny's classmates was called forward by Mr. Howard, an air of suspense seemed to be building. Finally, Johnny's name was called. Johnny began the slow walk to the auditorium stage, and everyone in the building knew that he would be handed a binder with that blank piece of paper.

All eyes were on Johnny as he made his way down the long aisle that divided students and family. As he climbed the stage steps and approached the podium, the faint chatter of student graduates, family and friends quickly faded and then came to a sudden halt. It was as if some unseen force had risen to command all present to silence. You could have heard the proverbial pin drop, and no one present had a sense of the coming storm that was about to shatter the quiet.

And then it happened. It began at first as a small murmuring. Then, like a cascading avalanche gaining speed with each passing second, it quickly evolved into a congregational chant. In spontaneous unison, everyone in the gymnasium was mouthing the words "Let him graduate, let him graduate, let him graduate …"

Holding the worthless graduation binder in hand, with Johnny now standing at his side, Mr. Howard looked over the audience, unsure of how to respond to this unexpected development. With the assembled crowd now standing and continuing to chant their plea, Mr. Sanders, the county school superintendent, rose and went to Mr. Howard's side, whispering something in his ear. Though everyone remained standing, a hush came over the crowd as Mr. Sanders returned to his seat. Everyone's attention was now focused on the high school principal as he nervously stood before them with Johnny's fate in his hands.

When he finally spoke, Mr. Howard's words were directed to Johnny but meant to be heard by everyone present. "Johnny, everyone knows of your athletic accomplishments during your school years. Everyone in the community thinks the world of you. We all know that math has been a most difficult challenge for you. Mr. Sanders, representing the county school's board of education, has suggested that if you can correctly solve one math problem on this stage, this day, you will receive your diploma and graduate with your class."

This was a development no one had anticipated. Everything hung in the balance, and everyone's attention was now focused, awaiting Mr. Howard's next words. What kind of problem was Johnny going to be given to solve?

Relief from the attending suspense was not long in coming as Mr. Howard, with only a moment's thought, proceeded to ask Johnny what the correct answer would be when you multiply the number eight by the number nine. Perhaps never in his experience, with all the last-minute shots or awaiting the final pitch of a game, had Johnny felt the pressure that this moment brought. The attention of everyone in the audience was focused like a laser on young Johnny. It was as if everyone were mentally willing the correct answer to his mind. Once again, across the entire auditorium, you could have heard a pin drop.

As Johnny stood on that stage considering the possible answers to the question, the seconds that passed seemed like an eternity. Finally, he responded by saying that he believed that eight times nine equaled seventy-two. Though no time actually elapsed, there was what seemed to be a long pause following his answer. Once again, it began quietly, but soon it became a loud, forceful chant in unison across the entire assembly: "Give him another chance, give him another chance, give him another chance ..."

There are several possible takeaways from this apocryphal story. The obvious one is that there may be times in your life when you are right and everyone in your circle hasn't got a clue. In this case, Johnny, despite his deficiencies in math, came up with the right answer. Everyone in the audience would have failed Mr. Howard's test. Sometimes, those we think may be knowledgeable about something, can actually have a blind spot of ignorance. Another lesson that may be learned is that no matter how many things a person does extremely well, just one weakness or failing can severely limit one's potential for growth.

But the lesson that I like best has to do with second chances, and therein lies another story.

No Big Deal

IT WAS ONE OF those busy summer days, early in my club management career, when one of my office staff rang my extension and asked if I had time to take a call. On the line was someone from the FBI asking to speak with me. Well, that is a call that most people don't necessarily welcome. It is also a call you can't put off.

In the conversation that followed, after identifying himself, the agent reaching out to me indicated he was working on the investigation of a particular individual. He was wondering if I could answer some questions about Jeff.

Jeff was a former employee. He had come to work for us during the latter part of his high school days and continued working at the club through most of his college years. His responsibilities included a variety of assignments, including clubhouse and course events setup.

He was one of the hundreds of young people who came to work for me over the years. One of my regrets is that over time I have retained little memory of so many of those kids. But this particular young man was not one of those. I remembered him well. The question now was why an FBI agent would be contacting me about Jeff?

I probably would not have paid any special attention to Jeff, or even remembered him, except for an incident that took place during one of our busy event weekends. Our team was doing an early Saturday morning reset of the facilities, preparing for the final day of our annual Men's Invitational Tournament. Everyone on the schedule was working to make the final day's experience everything it should be for the event participants … everyone, that is, except Jeff.

The crew was stretched, with much to do and not a lot of time to get it done. But where was Jeff? I called to see if he was on his way. As he answered the phone, his voice told me all I needed to know. It was obvious that my call was literally a wake-up call. All of the team had worked late the previous evening, and Jeff excused his absence by saying he had overslept. He apologized and promised to get to the club as soon as he possibly could.

Jeff showed up about twenty-five minutes later, forty-five minutes past the time he should have reported in. The work that needed to be done that morning was completed on time—everyone just had to work a little harder. I took a moment to call Jeff into my office right after we finished up. He was a good kid, a likable kid, with loads of potential. I wasn't just concerned about an employee not doing his job. I was disappointed in him and sensed a need to give a young man some counsel.

In the conversation that followed, I proceeded to let Jeff know that he had let the team down and that he needed to take his responsibilities more seriously. I wasn't posing rhetorical questions or looking to solicit any feedback. I just wanted to get my message across. He proceeded to excuse his tardiness by explaining that his alarm had failed to ring. I began to reinforce, with some additional emphasis, the need for Jeff to work at being more conscientious regarding his duties.

That is when the "big" mistake occurred, as Jeff interrupted me saying, "Bo, everything got done on time, it's no big deal." In retrospect, I must admit that I was close to my temper reaching the boiling point as I quickly responded to Jeff's unwelcome interruption. An employee can get fired for telling the boss what is—and what isn't—a big deal. I was direct in pointing out that it was I who signed his check, and when he was scheduled at a specific time, that was the time I expected him to be present and ready to work. Message delivered, Jeff quickly apologized.

From that day forward, Jeff was not only always on time but often arrived early and grew to become a valued member of the team. It was just a couple of years later, when a position for pool manager came open, that Jeff stopped by my office and asked if he could possibly be considered to fill the job. He was moving along in his college years and wanted a summer job with more responsibility and more pay.

I am not sure the call Jeff received that morning he overslept a few years earlier was the "wake-up" call that had brought about the change. But his performance from that point on reflected a different level of commitment, one that merited my consideration of his request. Although Jeff had no prior experience that would have prepared him for the responsibility, I had no hesitation in giving him a chance to take on the challenge. As I look back on the experience many years later, Jeff was one of the best pool managers I ever had.

So, now the FBI was on the line, inquiring about Jeff. I wondered what he could have done that warranted him being on their most wanted list. I didn't have to wait long for the answer as the agent explained that the purpose of his call was simply a part of the routine investigation process to verify employment and performance and provide a character reference.

Somehow, I had completely forgotten that Jeff was pursuing a degree in criminal justice. Following graduation, he was applying to work for the FBI. The final question that came in that conversation was simply whether I felt I could offer a positive reference for Jeff as a past employee. I was happy to be able to provide a positive recommendation for the "boy" I called and woke up that one Saturday morning, who was now a young man about to embark on his life's career.

Jeff and the fictional character Johnny in the previous story are just like us. No one is perfect.

We all make mistakes. Sometimes those mistakes are a "big deal." This life doesn't always provide another chance. Unlike in the movies, there are no retakes. Sometimes we get just one shot at taking advantage of an opportunity or making the best decision … and once that shot is taken, we have to live with the consequences.

But there is something that trumps the "big deal" moments in our life. Someone knew we would not always make the right, or the best, choices. Someone knew that we would fall and hurt ourselves … and sometimes hurt others. Someone knew we would need help. Someone has a plan and purpose for this world, and for us.

And just as there were those who loved and cared about that fictional character, Johnny, there is that Someone who loves and cares about each of us and has provided the way for us to have our second chance. He knew that just like Johnny, we would be deserving of nothing more than a blank sheet of paper in the "graduation binder" at the end of our life.

The real "big deal" is that, unlike Johnny, we are not dependent on a chanting crowd or a summer school class. Our second chance comes because of something that His Son did for us. The moment of coming to an understanding of why that is and what it can mean for each of us may be the most important moment we come to in this life.

A fuller understanding of that came to me early one morning ... and in a way that I least expected.

All in a Dream

I HAD FOUND MYSELF there many times before, seated comfortably in the chapel, waiting for the Sunday morning service to begin. Looking around the space, as I took in the setting, everything seemed as it always was. Rows of pews were neatly arranged that would seat the congregation of two hundred or more. A platform at the front of the chapel allowed for the elevated speaker's podium, with a short row of seats immediately behind that would accommodate those who would be on the program of this morning's service. Beyond those seats were the slightly elevated rows where the choir would be seated, with space that provided for the instrumental accompaniment of the organ and piano.

There was a routine that I had followed since the days of my boyhood when my family began going to church. I expected that this Sunday, this service, would be much like all the others that came before. At that moment I had no thought that this day was going to be something different ... something extraordinary.

It came as an abrupt interruption: the transition of a feeling of being completely at peace to a sudden feeling of panic. The change was initiated by a sudden awareness, confirmed from within, that I was the speaker on the program for today's service. Everyone seated in that chapel was waiting to hear the message that I had prepared for them to hear on this Sunday morning. The problem was, I had prepared nothing.

Speaking before a large group of people can come with some feeling of intimidation as you consider what you might have to share that could possibly be meaningful. But when you have given no thought or preparation to the task, intimidation can quickly transition to fear. My peaceful Sunday morning was no more.

Now aware that I was no longer to be the relaxed spectator, with as much nonchalance as I could muster, I stood and moved toward the speaker's platform. On the way, an impression of the topic of my presentation suddenly came to mind. I was to speak on the subject of the Atonement of Christ. I was not uncomfortable as a speaker. I had given numerous talks before on various topics, but never one on the Atonement. So in my mind, I had no preset outline that could be taken from previous speaking experiences. I was going to have to completely wing it and speak extemporaneously for twenty minutes on the subject.

As I took my place at the podium and looked out over the congregation, it was strange to see that there were few in attendance. There could have been no more than twenty souls scattered among the pews. I had a fleeting thought that this was good. If you are going to disappoint, possibly make a fool of yourself, the fewer to witness the spectacle, the better.

As I was taking a moment to gather my thoughts, I noticed that immediately to the right of the podium was a tall stack of books. There must have been more than a couple dozen neatly stacked books within reach, whose height rose to nearly match the height of the podium. It occurred to me that perhaps what I was meant to use as resource materials might be contained in those books.

But as I picked up and nervously paged through several of the volumes nearest the top of the stack, quickly looking for a marked place or card with scribble notes that might provide a guide for my comments, I was disappointed in finding nothing.

Then, as I turned my full attention back to the podium, the nightmare continued, with a twist. For in front of me on the podium, obstructing my full view of the congregation, there had suddenly appeared a vase of beautiful flowers. I carefully removed the vase and turned and placed it on the floor directly behind me.

Then, as I once again turned to face the congregation, I found that the podium was now no longer there. In its place was a music stand, like the one that a choir director would use while leading a choral group. Puzzled and frustrated by the continuing occurrence of the inexplicable, I wondered if the distractions would ever end. As I had done with the vase, I picked up the music stand, turned and placed it where it would normally be found in the choir seating area.

Once more, returning to face the congregation, I found the podium restored. To my surprise, I now found the chapel pews completely full. I recognized none who were in attendance, except some of my siblings who were seated directly before me on the front row. Before I could even take a moment to reflect on all these strange occurrences, I found the words of the message I was to give coming to my mind verbatim. Without any further thought, I began to speak. The message flowed from my lips as if I were reading from a text that had taken weeks of thoughtful preparation.

My remarks began with a detailed recounting of the story from the book of Daniel in the Old Testament where King Nebuchadnezzar had a disturbing dream, one that upon waking he could not recall. The book of scripture records that he calls forth the wise men of his kingdom to interpret his dream. The challenge put forth to them is not just in interpreting the dream but in recalling the dream itself, with the threat of death if they are unable to perform the task.

In the biblical account, following the failure of the king's wise men, Daniel comes forward and prophetically recalls the dream and provides an interpretation that he claims is true. The dream tells a story of a huge image whose body was made up of different elements, the head being made of finest gold, the breast and arms of silver, the belly and thighs of brass, legs of iron, and feet a mixture of iron and clay. In the king's dream, a stone cut out of a mountain without hands rolled forth and broke the various elements into pieces so that they became as the chaff on the summer threshing floors … and the wind carried them away so that they were to be found no more.

Daniel explained to the king that the image represented the kingdoms of man that would come forth and fall, one by one. He declared that the stone cut out of the mountain represented the rolling forth of the Kingdom of God, a kingdom that would not fall but would last forever.

My message continued by taking the congregation to the writings of the Gospel of John in the New Testament where, in the last hours of Christ's ministry, we find him retiring to an upper room for a "last supper" with his closest disciples, the twelve men he chose to be special witnesses of his ministry.

Several significant occurrences are recounted, including the coming betrayal by one of his own, the breaking of bread and passing of the cup of wine representing his body and blood that will be shed for them, and his instruction to do this often in remembrance of him.

As an example for them, Christ, in an act of humble servitude, washes their feet. He reminds them that they have not chosen him but that he has chosen them. He foretells his coming death and directs them to love one another. He then promises the coming of a "comforter" following his departure.

The message I had been given was simple, clear and unmistakable. The coming of the Kingdom of God had been foretold, and Jesus was the fulfillment of that prophecy. I concluded my remarks by quoting one of the most familiar passages from the scriptures, "For God so loved the world that he gave his only begotten Son, that whosoever believeth in him should not perish, but have everlasting life."

I suddenly awoke with a start. What I had just experienced was all in a dream.

The place where dreams reside is frequently like the mist that disappears with the morning light. This was nothing like that. Upon my awakening, I had total recall and a clear sense of what I had just experienced, with none of the rapid loss of details that often occurs when coming out of a deep dream state.

As I lay still in my bed, I sought to revisit in my mind the strange experience that had just unfolded, but with it being the very early hours of the morning, I fairly quickly began to fall back asleep. I had no sooner drifted back into that restful state than I experienced a full replay of what had been given to me in the first encounter. It was as if I were watching a rerun of a program that I had previously viewed numerous times. In exactly the same sequence, with the same script repeated word-perfect, the dream came to me again.

The scenario played out twice more. As soon as I would fall back into sleep, it was as if a replay button were being pushed, with me once again walking through the dream sequence, exactly as before. Upon the conclusion of the fourth viewing experience of this most unusual dream, more than an hour had passed. It was now nearing 4 a.m. I was physically and mentally exhausted but lay completely awake, unable now to return to sleep.

My mind was active and alert. The impression was very strong that this strange and powerful dream was not my mind conjuring up something from my subconscious. I was being given something with purpose and for a reason. Upon rising, I once more brought the details of this dream to mind. As soon as I was able to sit down at my desk that morning, I wrote down the recollection of what I had been given.

For some time, I pondered what the meaning of it all was. Obviously, the message was a testament of the divinity of Jesus, that He is The Christ. His coming was prophesied. His life was a fulfillment of those prophecies. The men He chose to be his Apostles were to be the special witnesses who continued his work, testifying that He lived, that He died on a Roman cross for us and rose from the tomb.

But what of all the most unusual happenings that occurred in the dream, the several strange occurrences as I was attempting to speak to the congregation? God has always spoken to his prophets, but he also speaks to the hearts of men and women. I won't pretend to be a Daniel, but permit me to share the interpretation of the dream God put into my heart that night.

It is not unusual for God to choose individuals to fulfill his purposes who are ill equipped and unprepared to do his work. In this dream, I was ill prepared to complete the assignment given. Oh, of course, I had knowledge of the Atonement. But I had never in my experience prepared notes for an organized and well-thought-out presentation on the topic.

The stack of books by the podium, I believe, represents the learning of the world that was available to me. The lack of anything of use among those volumes that I could see led me to understand that God intended for me to say what he wanted me to say. It was to be his words given ... not mine.

The strange appearance of the vase of flowers and the replacing of the podium with the music stand represent the things of the world that could come and distract from God's message and interfere in the work he would have done. In the dream, when the various distractions were removed, the learning of the world found in the books having been set aside, and the giver of the message was standing in faith, ready to speak ... the chapel was full of people and the message that God intended came verbatim out of my mouth, without any hesitation and with no thought given.

The message of the dream seems clear. When we set aside the distractions of the world and seek to lean on God's understanding, he will give us the words to speak. The promised comforter will be there to bear witness to the truth. Just as in Jesus' ministry, those who have ears hear. They are ready and prepared to listen.

In my youth, I learned the stories of Jesus. I have heard the testimonies of many regarding the truthfulness of his Gospel. I have prayed and have had many prayers answered.

But I never prayed for this dream. Somewhat like King Nebuchadnezzar, it was just given to me.

Never had a dream come to me in the way that this dream came, with such clarity and power for recall, repeated four times, with each time the experience of the retelling exactly as before. It would have been possible for my mind to conjure up a dream once … even a second time, but four times with it being an exact encore performance tells me this wasn't really a dream. It was something more.

And I don't believe it was given to me, just for me.

Like every other good thing that God may do for us in our lives, there is an attending obligation to share that moment. There are times when those things are given to us in our waking hours.

Sometimes those moments to be shared come to us … all in a dream.

The Rest of the Story

It was just another event reception, like so many that I had attended or been responsible for organizing over the years. I was very familiar with the drill and, as was my usual routine, I arrived just a few minutes past the announced time when I knew guests would begin arriving. I was still considered a relative newcomer, having been a member of the community for less than two years, so coming across several familiar faces that I recognized helped make the mixing and mingling portion of the evening less uncomfortable.

The charity golf outing being promoted was a significant regional event, well supported by a number of community leaders. Each year nearly a quarter of a million dollars was raised for a good cause. The purpose of the evening's gathering was to recognize in advance the corporate sponsors who were engaged in helping make this year's event a success. As our club had been the site of the event since its inception nearly twenty-five years earlier, as the club's general manager, I had been asked to be present and to share a few remarks at the end of the evening.

My time on the program would amount to something less than ten minutes. Usually on occasions like these, I would provide some updates on what was happening at the club, share an entertaining anecdote and conclude my remarks by expressing appreciation for being able to be a part of such a positive, noteworthy community cause. All of the energy put forth in this annual event supported a national organization well known for its role in helping match children in need with loving families. I had two siblings who had become adoptive parents, which brought some personal feelings to the table as I would work on this event each year.

I was comfortable and enjoyed speaking in front of groups. As the time approached for me to take the podium, I thought this would be just like many of the other occasions where some brief remarks were made and soon forgotten. I had no idea that this evening's experience would be not just memorable, but one that would forever change how I thought about life's opportunities and challenges. As the preceding speakers on the program each rose in turn to share a few thoughts, my mind drifted away to moments of an earlier time and place in my life.

In the second semester of my junior year of high school, every Tuesday and Thursday at twelve noon I would find myself spending forty terrifying minutes with one of my teachers and two fellow students. I am not sure which was worse in those driver's education sessions—being behind the wheel or sitting helplessly in the back seat. At the time, I truly had no idea what degree of anxiety our teacher must have felt. However, years later, after having been in the passenger seat as an instructor for my children as they learned to drive, I was able to gain some perspective on the experience. The first ride on the highest, fastest, twisting and looping roller coaster could have nothing on the first drive on the road with my oldest daughter as she was learning to drive a stick shift. I think you get the picture.

I am not sure why our driver's education teacher turned on the radio during our driving sessions. Maybe he just wanted some sort of distraction to allow us to forget that we were in for forty minutes of mortal danger. Perhaps he just had a predilection for Paul Harvey's daily radio program. But as my fellow students and I gradually became more comfortable behind the wheel, I was able to focus less on the present danger and more on the sharing of Harvey's daily perspective on current events.

Paul Harvey was one of the great commentators of our day. He brought to the radio what newspaper journalists bring to the editorial page. He had a way of interestingly bringing reason into explaining what was happening in our world and some thought about how a person should be seeing it all. His commentary sounded as if he were reading it right off a prepared script, which he no doubt was. As he moved along with the sharing of his thoughts for the day, he would periodically announce the progress through the prepared text … page two, page three and so on.

He would often introduce a person of significance by first providing some lesser-known background details of an event that had taken place.

After "setting the table" in that manner, he would then continue by saying, "Now for the rest of the story ..." He would then proceed to reveal the historic figure who had been the key player in the story he had just recounted. It was his way of letting folks have an experience of becoming acquainted with the history surrounding an event or place, with the discovery of something more than what appeared to most of us on the surface.

Now, as I was about to take the stage at our event sponsor's reception, I had prepared to share a version of one of my "rest of the story" experiences ... and I had no idea why.

It all began earlier that day, a couple of hours before I was to leave for the fifteen-minute drive to the downtown site of the evening's reception. As I took a few minutes to consider what might be included in my presentation, the story of Rose came to mind. I had not thought about her for many years, but I enjoyed once more going over in my mind the meeting of a stranger in a department store ... that turned out to be more than just a chance encounter.

After running back over the story in my mind, I quickly rejected the possible use of that experience in my prepared comments for that evening's event. It was a wonderful story, but I couldn't find the way to make it relevant for those who would be present at the reception. I quickly turned my mind to other possible approaches.

However, every time my mind began to go down another path, the story of Rose returned once more to my thoughts. I must have replayed the story in my mind several times when I finally realized that, for whatever reason, that story was the one I was meant to share in my presentation. Having had similar previous experiences, I was comfortable following what seemed to be a definite prompting of what I was supposed to do on this occasion. It still made no sense, but there was no doubt that this was what was supposed to happen.

So it was that I found myself waiting patiently for my turn to speak, half-listening to the several individuals who preceded me on the evening's program. I had just completed taking one last time to walk through in my mind my experience with Rose, when the speaker who was scheduled to immediately precede me on the program took the stand. Though I should not have been surprised by what followed, as she began sharing her prepared remarks, I quickly understood why I had been impressed to share the story of Rose.

I had the impression that the organization that was the recipient of this fundraising effort was all about promoting the process of adoption. However, in the short presentation that was being made, I became aware of the foster care program that had become a key part of the children's services that this group provided. What I was able to share in my story of Rose, and her experience as a foster child in my parents' home, was a perfect and fitting conclusion to the evening in having everyone more informed in a special way as to how foster care had the potential to change the life of a child.

So, there was a second act to what I thought was a warm and inspirational experience from many years ago. It would have been worthy of one of Paul Harvey's "rest of the story" commentaries. However, perhaps the lesson isn't isolated to this two-part play with a group of people being able to come away with a better understanding of a particular aspect of service to others.

Are the things that happen to us in life just random acts? Is what happened with my Rose experience just coincidental? In my mind, I have no doubt that what occurred was known long before it happened. What took place on that special evening involved more than twenty years of moments in time in the making. Perhaps the real lesson is that, though we have our agency and make our decisions, there is a purpose to this existence, and there is someone who knows all that is to come.

I have always had a thought that I was a person who took care to be in control ... not necessarily of others, but of myself. I was that person who worked at being self-reliant and not depending on anyone else. I was the confident one whose knowledge and ability would be sufficient to do whatever I set out to do.

My Rose experience told me that I need to be less concerned with that. There is someone else who has that responsibility, and the more I come to understand that—understand him—the more productive and purposeful a life I will be able to experience.

Indeed, as Paul Harvey would say, "And that's the rest of the story." However, I would suggest, and one might well conclude, that for us in this life, that's the only story.

Another Book on the Shelf

I WAS JUST A few weeks away from retiring and what would be my last day on the job, when I received the news of the passing of a good friend of mine. Bill had gone to sleep the previous evening ... and just didn't wake up. It happens.

We tend to take so much in life for granted. At the beginning of each day, we get up in the morning and flip a switch on the wall that will provide light, turn the knob of a faucet that brings us running water and push a button that will start our vehicle. Most days, most of those things happen. But on occasion, we experience the unexpected.

So can it be with the passing of a family member, friend or acquaintance. We rise every morning with the expectation that those we know, and those who are closest to us, are still with us. Why is it that, so often, the unexpected loss comes to us as such a shock? After all, we all come to understand that having been brought into this life, one day it will be our time to leave.

I always loved family reunions, the one day a year that my dad's family would all come together. There was much anticipation of seeing everyone at those gatherings, but there was also a certain amount of sadness that always came with the experience. At the end of a day of visiting, sharing an enjoyable meal and fun and games, there always came the time of parting. No one wanted to be the first to leave, but being the last to depart came with its own feeling of loss. Those were the feelings that accompanied Bill's time of leaving us.

At the family's request, we were able to have a celebration of life gathering for Bill at the club, a place he loved and had shared so many good memories with family and friends. It was a beautiful spring afternoon. The temperature was not ideal, but the cool weather was countered by a day with some sunshine and the warmth of the hearts of those in attendance.

The participants in the program included Bill's daughter, two sons and a longtime business partner. The concluding speaker on the program was Bill's lifelong best friend. The thoughts and remembrances shared were a mixture of both humorous and touching stories of the life of a husband, father, businessperson, community leader and friend.

I had worked closely with Bill in my time at the club. For more than half of my thirteen years at Egypt Valley, he had served on the board of directors, with two of those years in the role of club president—my boss. We had both spent time working with others to see the club through some challenging times. I thought I knew the man. I was wrong.

Bill would often stop by my office. Sometimes we would discuss and work through a little bit of business. Usually, we would end up talking about sports and politics … always much more sports than politics. We both loved sports of all sorts, but we had quite different leanings relative to how we might see the solution to the challenges of the world and current events.

Being more from the South, I never understood how he could get so excited about a game of hockey, but when we found the conversation drifting into college basketball or pro football, Bill could end up being late for his afternoon tee time. In his college days, he had been a quarterback, but his best friends might tell you that he would have made a better linebacker, and Bill might have agreed with that assessment. Though deep inside he had a soft heart, he possessed a tough, no-nonsense mentality.

In retrospect, the interesting thing to me is that Bill never allowed any of the differences in how we thought about things to make a difference in our relationship. It seems to me that at the end of the day, he made our friendship more important than anything else that could have been a distraction to finding common ground and making things happen. I knew all of this and more. However, as I listened to Bill's children, followed by his long-time law partner, the picture came more into focus and became ever clearer, and I found that there was so much more that I didn't know about the life he had lived. Then Denny got up to speak.

Bill had many friends, and several very close friends. But Denny was his best friend. I would get to see a different side of Bill every year at our club's

Men's Invitational, when Denny came into town to be his golf partner for the three-day event. My first memory of Denny was at a casino party evening on the third day of one of those invitationals, when Bill and Denny sat at my blackjack table all evening. I was the dealer, and they were the slightly inebriated guys who just loved getting together and having a good time. Well, to be honest, there were times when slightly inebriated might not have been the most accurate description of those two.

Ever after that event, whenever Denny would see me, his greeting wasn't, "Hey, Bo!"; it was "Hey, Boooooo!!!" Seeing those two enjoying that annual event over the years became one of those things I really looked forward to, and it provided me with some very memorable moments.

As Denny rose to speak, I wondered how long he would be able to keep his emotions in check. As expected, his remarks were not lengthy. He managed well the sharing of how he and Bill had got to know each other and some of their most humorous experiences over the years. Their history went all the way back to their college days, so there was plenty of material to work with. I knew as he was speaking that I would, over time, forget some of the funny stories, but Denny shared something that I did not expect and immediately knew I would not forget.

The revelation was that over their lifetime, he and Bill would speak with each other nearly every day. Denny noted that the closeness of the relationship was such that whenever Bill would call the house, Denny's wife would call out to him, "Denny, it's your codependent on the phone!" To me, that was unbelievable. I had many friends over the years. I couldn't imagine having a friend I would talk with every day. It was just another reminder of something of significance about Bill I knew nothing about, and as I reflected on that a bit more, I wondered how many other things there were about Bill that I had not known.

We all have people come in and out of our lives. The reality is, we actually know very little about them. We may think we do, but for the most part, that's an illusion. What we mostly have discovered are the things we have in common or the points where differences exist. But all that amounts to is the tip of the iceberg. For most of us, their story is something like a book on the shelf that is never taken down … and never opened.

The saying goes that the person who can read but doesn't is no better off than the person who can't read. The stories of all the people in our lives are being written. How often are we taking time to pick up the books off the shelf and caring enough to do a little reading?

But there is a more important question ... one I would offer you, the reader, for your consideration. The stories of *your* life are also being written. Are you taking the time to catch the "sweet spot" moments found within and use them to help you better understand the purpose and meaning in your life?

Or are you leaving the book of your life's experience on the shelf to be left unnoticed, unappreciated and of no benefit to anyone, including yourself? Nothing more than just another book on the shelf.

The world is full of those books ... the kind of which we need no more.

Epilogue

IT WAS MONDAY, late afternoon, the first day my management replacement was on the job, and my responsibility at the club was nearing its end. The thirteen years at Egypt Valley Country Club represented the last stop in a club management career that spanned four decades. My better half and I were on our way out to an early dinner when I noticed a call coming through. I could see that it was Krista, one of our best friends, calling. With a sideways glance I made the comment, "Hey, it's your codependent calling." Denny's story about himself and Bill's close relationship was fresh in my mind.

Following the call, it was suggested that I owed Krista an explanation for that remark. I wasn't sure that was necessary because at our house, Krista was our Denny. A day without a call from her was an unimaginable thing. But I noted the request.

The call was an urgent plea to stop by the club. Krista had a family member who thought she'd left her purse at the club over the weekend, and she wondered if we could make a quick detour and retrieve it for her. It was on the way, so in just a few minutes, we came through the club entry gate and onto the property.

I pulled up to the front entrance and entered the clubhouse. As I stepped through the door, I heard voices when there should have been none. The club was closed on Mondays. The voices seemed to be coming from the upstairs ballrooms. About that time, a couple of my staff leaders appeared on the mezzanine. I thought, *How nice, the staff is throwing a welcoming party for the new manager.*

Susie, my comptroller, motioned for me to come up the stairs. I thought, well yes, it would be appropriate for me to make an appearance. At the same time, I was a little aggravated that I had not officially been included in the welcoming celebration.

When I reached the top of the stairs, I could see into the small ballroom, and as expected, immediately recognized some of my former team leaders.

It wasn't until I stepped into the room that the realization came upon me that I was the victim of an elaborate ruse. A surprise retirement dinner had secretly been arranged for me. Somehow, the talkative people in my life had managed for weeks to keep the surprise a secret.

It was a memorable evening with a wonderful dinner prepared by our culinary team. It was an enjoyable "last supper" with my friends, those who were most responsible for making so many good things happen during my time at the club. Following dinner, there was a short informal program, the viewing of a special video that had been prepared by my team and the presenting of some parting gifts.

One of the gifts was a small book of pictorial memories from my time at the club. Interspersed among the photos were a number of "Wish you well" messages from board and committee members with whom I had served over the years. It was a most thoughtful gift, one that I knew I would always treasure.

It was just a few days later that I found myself taking some time to sit down and enjoy a more thorough read-through of that volume. The turn of each page was like a walk back through time. The experience was reminiscent of the time long ago when I'd spent hours paging through my parents' photo album. Once again, there was a bit of sadness at the moments past and faces possibly never to be seen again.

As I turned to the final page, I found myself experiencing what some say happens in the last moments of your life. My time, the years at the club, flashed before me, and then, as if by the closing of a door, the view of it all was suddenly taken from me. It was time for me to move on. Another chapter in my life was finished.

As I read the words on the last page, a comforting feeling of peace came over me. There was only one source from which such a fitting finish to that little book could have been arranged. It was He who had been responsible for all the "sweet spot" moments that had come along in my life. He saw to it that I would have one more. Somehow, arranged for me as the final missive in that special book was one penned for me by my good friend Bill.

Found there were the usual words of congratulations for one about to retire and some reflective thoughts shared by Bill of our time working together. He noted that we were able to face and overcome a number of challenges, becoming friends along the way. Bill likened my challenge of having come into the club as a manager to that of a college coach challenged with the rebuilding of a failed program. That was appropriate, as our conversations always seemed to end up tied in with our favorite topic … sports.

Near the bottom of that last page were found his final words of farewell for me.

"Please keep in touch."

Bill must have penned that last message about a month before my retirement, with the book I was holding in my hands going to press just a couple of weeks before he passed away.

Life is truly about the moments. I like to think that, in part, the writing of this book is just another way of showing appreciation for Bill, and for so many of the others who have been an important part of my life.

I'll be doing my best to "stay in touch."

Just One Last Thought

WELL, THE WORLD didn't need another book, just to sit on one's shelf and collect dust. Hopefully, you didn't find this one to be one of those.

I wrote the stories of some of my "sweet spot" moments so that I would not forget them nor the lessons they helped bring to my understanding. My final thought for you is that you too have these kinds of moments come along nearly every day.

Like me, you may not have made a habit of keeping a journal. You may not be that person who is continually taking pictures or making video recordings.

If that is the case, just keep a notebook or writing pad handy and take a few moments each day to consider what may have happened on that day that you never want to forget.

You will be surprised what you'll be able to accumulate in just a short period of time. The sad thing is that much of it will disappear, be forgotten and lost forever if you do nothing.

I found the three Rs—Reflection, Recognition and Reconciliation—helpful in turning my notes into memories with meaning. However, there is one more "R" that I discovered along the way that can come with the "sweet spot" experience. Redemption.

I once had a good friend offer up a somewhat challenging question. Ben was my sous chef. However, friends and fellow staff members always referred to him by his nom de guerre: Kingsley. He and I would occasionally enjoy some conversation on a variety of topics. Those conversations would frequently venture into our contrasting philosophical views on politics and religion. Nothing was off limits. One afternoon, as we were enjoying discussing some of the mysteries of the universe, Kingsley asked me if I could possibly define the purpose of life in just one word. After a moment of thought, I responded that I didn't think one word would be enough, but maybe two could get the job done.

I told Kingsley my two words would simply be "Become better."

Redemption is the moment of transformation. It's where we begin allowing a true principle that we have come to understand put us on the path to one of the "become better" places in our life.

My best wishes for you on your journey of finding the moments and discovering your "sweet spots."

My hope is that in the end, you don't just settle for the ordinary ... but that your life's experience is one that is found to be extraordinary.

About the Author

Bo Picklesimer was born and spent his early childhood years in Kentucky. After a family move away from Appalachia, many of the experiences of his youth took place in small-town environments in rural Ohio. Early mentoring influences drove an interest in entrepreneurism and the field of financial management.

By the age of thirty, he had developed his own small-office accounting practice, been a controller for a multi-company operation, gained experience working for a professional accountancy firm and cofounded a restaurant group. Following a career in the field of private club management that spanned four decades, Bo writes and speaks about the lessons to be learned from everyday life.

Whether speaking in an intimate small group setting or to audiences of a thousand or more, Bo most enjoys the interaction with people and the exchange of life-changing ideas. Active over the years in community and hospitality industry leadership, Bo is a certified club manager and a past president of the Greater Michigan Club Managers Association. An interest in reading, particularly history, and music occupies some of his leisure moments.

Made in the USA
Monee, IL
16 January 2023